Homespun Style

Selina Lake
Homespun
Style

Words by Joanna Simmons
Photography by Debi Treloar

RYLAND
PETERS
& SMALL
LONDON NEW YORK

SENIOR DESIGNER
Megan Smith

COMMISSIONING EDITOR
Annabel Morgan

LOCATION RESEARCH
Selina Lake and Jess Walton

HEAD OF PRODUCTION
Patricia Harrington

ART DIRECTOR
Leslie Harrington

EDITORIAL DIRECTOR
Julia Charles

STYLING Selina Lake

First published in 2012
by Ryland Peters & Small
20–21 Jockey's Fields
London WC1R 4BW
and
519 Broadway, 5th Floor
New York, NY 10012
www.rylandpeters.com

Text copyright
© Selina Lake 2012
Design and photographs
copyright © Ryland Peters
& Small 2012

10 9 8 7 6 5 4 3

ISBN 978-1-84975-201-5

A CIP record for this book
is available from the British
Library.

Library of Congress CIP
data has been applied for.

Printed and bound in China

contents

Anyone in search of unique, innovative and
sustainable ideas for every room in the house will
love homespun style. It is a look that celebrates
customized furniture and hand-crafted pieces, for a
home that is quirky, colourful and gloriously eclectic.

OPPOSITE Wooden
chairs painted cheerful
colours flank a table
draped with vintage
fabric and lace, with
pretty handkerchiefs
knotted together as
bunting. The cake stand
is made from teacups.
BELOW LEFT This
bedroom has a colourful
patchwork theme, with
cushions and a wall of
paper swatches.

introduction

If you are crazy about colour, fascinated by craft and would rather paint a
junk-store chair than buy a new one, then you will love homespun style.
A look that believes homes should be an expression of our tastes, travels and
experiences, the homespun look is welcoming, warm and unpretentious. Rooms
are brimming with homemade pieces and individual touches; restored flea-
market finds and one-off treasures. They are studded with colour and dotted
with fresh, fun patterns on cushions, lampshades and throws.

Featuring beautiful and inspiring homes around the world, homespun style
reflects our growing love of craft and creativity. It shows how objects made by
talented craftspeople, or modified with a needle and thread or a lick of paint,
will bring soul to any scheme. In addition, this cosy, relaxed look revels in the
design possibilities of recycling and reusing, with the flea market – not the chain
stores – the richest hunting ground for furniture that packs an original punch.
Best of all, homespun style throws out the interiors rule book, inviting you to
enjoy and experiment with colours, textiles and eye-catching displays, creating
rooms that bring joy to you and your family every day.

elements

modern craft

Give your rooms unique homespun
personality with one-off creations,
handmade accessories and plenty
of easy-to-stitch trimmings.

THIS PAGE Colourful cushions and a knitted blanket take a bench from dull to homespun in an instant. Pretty trimmings are another cornerstone of this look – here used to cheer up a lampshade and table – as are informal displays of postcards, single panels of wallpaper and quirky paintings on walls.

modern craft is all about flexing your creative muscles as you make, modify or completely remodel the furniture and accessories in your home. Skill and crafting experience are not essential, but imagination helps. Have fun!

OPPOSITE A simple shelving unit made from old floorboards provides space for displaying vintage floral china. Sewing kit, including thread, fabric and ribbons, looks beautiful stored among the crockery.

ABOVE LEFT Colourful cotton is a vital starting point for creating homespun style. These vintage reels in candy-coloured shades and complete with their pretty original storage box are a treasured find.

ABOVE CENTRE Colourful crocheted doilies look great whether piled high or taped to walls to make a crafty display.
ABOVE RIGHT Keep pins to hand in a cute vintage-look pincushion.

As the name suggests, the homespun looks relies on homemade ingredients. If you want to inject personality, warmth and comfort into your home, there is no better way than with a piece that you have decorated, adapted or even made. But while crafting used to be all about dying arts and complicated techniques, modern craft is not difficult. Forget spinning yarn or whittling wood – it is about simple tweaks and easy ideas to brighten up the pieces you already own, or personalize what you have bought. It doesn't need to be tricky or complex. Anyone can stitch buttons onto a cushion cover to give it a fresh look. Anyone can give an old chair a bright coat of fresh paint. It's about getting stuck in, rediscovering the pleasure of working with your hands and rethinking how you decorate your home.

There has been a huge resurgence of interest in crafting in the last decade. Go online and you will find hundreds of websites and blogs celebrating modern craft. There are thousands of easy-to-follow projects out there, too, employing every kind of crafting technique, from simple sewing to crochet and knitting; from upholstery to furniture restoration. Plus, with hundreds of craft stores online, it's never been easier to find materials.

Of course, making things is nothing new. People have always created pieces for their homes, often using traditional techniques that they have modified to fit their needs. In the past, we were making out of necessity, but today we make things simply because we want to. It is a way to express ourselves, to reconnect with our creative side and produce something unique and personal.

So where does this new fascination with craft come from? It may be born of the tough economic times we live in. If you have bought an inexpensive junk-store piece and turned it into something lovely with a pot of paint, you may wonder why you ever bought flat-pack furniture at all.

There's also something more emotional behind our rediscovered love of craft. Most of us watched our mothers or grandmothers knitting or sewing when we were little. We may have worn sweaters that they had made, or snuggled up under a blanket they had crocheted. The previous generation was willing to repair and restore furniture, too – perhaps granddad did it in his shed? People cared for their possessions in a time before the disposable, throwaway culture we know today. It is this respect for our home and its ingredients that we are all reconnecting with now.

If you are inspired to get crafting but are not quite sure where you should start, consider enrolling on a course at a craft workshops in your area.

LEFT Confident colours and vibrant patterns give the homespun look both energy and personality. This pretty bobble-edged scarf combines both.

ABOVE LEFT Colourful, playful trimmings are a classic homespun ingredient that will brighten up a lampshade, cushion or throw.

THIS PAGE Decorative but ordered, this workstation contains lots of clever homespun elements. Walls are painted white as a backdrop to the very modern neon pink on chairs, lampshades and mats. A mix of pieces adorns the wall, from plates to postcards, while lighting on coloured flex/cord is both funky and flexible.

ABOVE This work table, dedicated to crafting, is both pretty and practical. Buttons are stored in glass jars and rolls of wrapping and wallpaper held in a simple bin. A plain pinboard has been personalized with wallpaper and its frame painted bright purple.

LEFT Keeping materials like fabric, cotton, ribbon or wool on display has several benefits: they are easily accessible, and also, by being visible, provide inspiration and an unexpected decorative touch, too.

OPPOSITE ABOVE This vintage drawer unit, originally intended for use in a kitchen, makes fabulous storage for materials such as trimmings, buttons and beads. The plastic drawers make it easy to see what is stored within.

OPPOSITE BELOW The tiny materials used to embellish soft furnishings in a homespun home can easily get lost or scattered. Here, jars, boxes and old tins and their lids keep small beads and buttons ordered yet visible.

It doesn't matter if you are not skilled with a knitting needle, though. Modern craft is accessible to all via the thousands of independent makers producing exciting, one-off designs. Their work is available online through sites such as etsy.com, while others reach their market through crafts stores and fairs. Check local listings for details of upcoming events.

Modern craft is not about perfection or precision but about personality. Pieces that are funny, colourful or just plain quirky will bring pleasure and a light touch to your home. They are central to the homespun look and an antidote to the bland, mass-produced items available from chain stores or shopping malls. Whether you are sticking on a sequin or trimming a curtain, modern craft will make your home unique, bursting with colour, pattern and energy.

LEFT Homespun style takes a modern approach to craft, rejecting tricky techniques in favour of simple makes that will quickly brighten your home. Here, fabric strips are tied together to make pom-poms and plain paper shades are embellished with ribbon and paper flowers.

BELOW Storage for your crafting paraphernalia need not be expensive. Here, it is stored in an old wooden box, picked up at a flea market.

OPPOSITE ABOVE LEFT Postcards mounted on wallpaper remnants are stuck to this wall using patterned and coloured tape to make a relaxed, collage-style artwork.

OPPOSITE ABOVE RIGHT Homemade cushions and soft toys in pretty fabrics bring cute personality to a child's bed.

OPPOSITE BELOW LEFT A simple stuffed heart, stitched from fabric offcuts, adds to this informal display of pattern-rich pieces.

OPPOSITE BELOW RIGHT A quirky handmade doily owl hangs up among other treasures.

homespun tip Fabric remnants can be used to make simple pom-pom decorations. Simply cut the material into strips, bind them all at the top with brightly coloured yarns, then suspend them from hooks.

colour &
pattern

Embrace bold combinations and bright
tones, teaming strong blocks of colour
with pattern in various shades to bring
interest and depth to every room.

colour & pattern are central to the homespun look. From retro prints in candy shades to ethnic textiles; from patterned wallpaper to pretty woven rugs, work it in around your home for rooms bursting with colour and life.

OPPOSITE A canvas, depicting ethereal swallows and flower motifs, painted by the owner of this home sits on a mantelpiece. It is deliberately a work-in-progress, for a relaxed, unpretentious feel.

ABOVE LEFT A pile of neatly folded fabric swatches in a dazzling rainbow of shades.
ABOVE CENTRE Fine tissue-paper decorations bring contrasting bright hues to this lime green wall.

ABOVE RIGHT Wallpaper, both new and vintage, comes in a vibrant array of shades and patterns. Stored upright in a bin or tub, it is easy to appreciate how various tones and designs work together.

In recent decades, with minimalism spreading the gospel of less is more, the perfectly simple white room with pared-back furniture combination has proved popular. And you can understand why. It is calming and also very easy to pull off, but what this kind of interior lacks, quite obviously, is colour, life and originality. For this very reason, minimalism is falling out of favour in many homes today. It seems that we increasingly crave a more individual, interesting and exuberant style for our homes, something that speaks of who we are and how we live, and that is where the homespun look comes in.

We all respond to colours in nature – a gorgeous flower or a bird's dazzling plumage – and the same is true of colour in the home. It can energize, excite and delight. It can make a cold room feel warm or a large space feel intimate. That said, it may seem too bold to inject egg-yolk yellow or magenta into your rooms. So take things slowly and think about your scheme. While the homespun look is relaxed, it is not chaotic. It takes a little planning!

Most homespun homes follow a wonderfully simple recipe. It starts with a neutral shell. White walls are the fail-safe way to anchor bright colours and busy patterns, helping them to stand out

without crowding a space. For those nervous about using colour, painting your walls a pale neutral hue is a reassuringly no-risk strategy, too. You are not committing to bold colour on every wall; you can simply introduce it in the form of soft furnishings, lampshades and ceramics, which can easily be repositioned or replaced.

With the background in place, adding colour and pattern is easy. Begin with just a splash, perhaps on a single chair, then use the same tone in a handful of places, to subtly theme your space. A feature wall of turquoise or an alcove hung with vintage wallpaper has a place in the homespun scheme, too. If art is your passion, hang colourful

Cornflower
Navy
Indigo
Cobalt
Prussian
Harebell
Sky
Powder

OPPOSITE ABOVE LEFT These chairs have had only their backs and seats painted. The legs are left as bare wood for a creative, original look. A board painted with blue paint that acts like a blackboard sits on the table — handy for writing messages or lists on, but colourful, too.

OPPOSITE ABOVE RIGHT This bright and beautiful floral fabric, designed by Bluebellgray, stands out against the muted, powdery pastel green walls.

OPPOSITE BELOW A bright, patterned chair can be teamed with a patterned cushion for a layered, visually lush effect.

LEFT These stair risers here have been painted a deep blue, with the names of classic blue paint shades stencilled on each.

BELOW Coloured units and assorted vintage tiles give this simple kitchen its own personality, while a handful of fresh flowers from the garden inject subtle, natural colour.

paintings in arresting arrangements and treat your floors to patterned rugs. The homespun look also celebrates flexibility, so rather than buy a sofa or armchair in a strong shade, brighten up an existing, neutral piece with cushions, crocheted blankets or throws. When you tire of the mix, you can simply swap them around or give them a makeover with braiding or pom-poms.

When it comes to choosing your palette, be bold. Remember the bright, uncomplicated colours that filled our childhood paintboxes? Sunshine yellow, sea blue, tomato red and darkest green. These are unapologetically strong tones, but when teamed with plenty of calming white they can be invigorating and interesting to live with. Alternatively, try using them against a knocked-back version of themselves – a touch of brilliant emerald punctuating a powdery, pale green, for example.

RIGHT Rather than a wall papered in one single design, here small sheets of patterned paper have been pasted directly onto the wall to create a colourful, patchwork effect.
FAR RIGHT Bursting with colour, this iconic Hang It All coat rack, designed by Charles Eames, fits in perfectly with a homespun scheme.
BELOW A passion for stylized Sixties and Seventies fabrics is clearly visible in this colourful bedroom, where patchwork cushions and a dress made from floral fabric from that period look striking against the white walls.

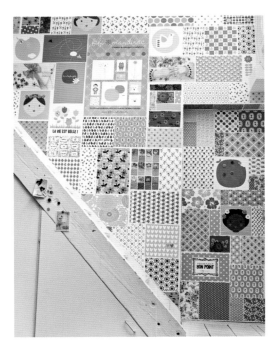

Pattern – on wallpaper, textiles and rugs – brings further interest to your space. There is a pattern to suit every taste out there, too, from old-fashioned chintz to Seventies geometrics; tiny florals to bold, large-repeat designs. How you use it is entirely up to you. A patterned cushion instantly brightens a neutral armchair. A decorative cloth can conceal a tired-out table and beautifully revive it.

If you crave pattern on your walls, wallpaper is the obvious choice, but why not give it extra homespun style by pasting a patchwork of patterns onto one wall. Remember covering your bedroom walls with posters when you were a teenager? Take the same approach, but this time using wallpaper offcuts, pictures, postcards or even wrapping paper. Don't be afraid to clash colours and designs either, but beware of overload. A large patterned wallpaper is enough embellishment for one wall; pictures hung over it could tip the look from bold to busy.

homespun tip When shopping for fabric, think about scale before you reject any piece. A retro 1970s curtain might be overpowering hung in your living room, but it could look fantastic as cushion covers.

OPPOSITE Create a standout feature wall by pasting one side of a room with a paper that combines vibrant colour with a large-scale repeat pattern – in this case, the wallpaper is designed by Amy Butler.
RIGHT A small alcove filled with travel souvenirs is framed by colourful paper.
BELOW Upholstering this sofa and armchair in a mix of primary-coloured corduroy gives it a strong, confident look, which can be tweaked by moving the cushions around.

ABOVE You don't need to use a lot of colour to make a bold statement. Here, only the inside of the door and a wooden bench have been painted bright egg-yolk yellow, to look striking without being overpowering.
RIGHT Simple wooden picture frames are painted neon pink and draped with mini lights, to add personality.

customize & recycle

Do the right thing, for the planet and your home, and discover the delights of recycling! From furniture to wallpaper and textiles, second-hand pieces come with lashings of homespun character.

customize & recycle It makes more than simply ecological sense to use second-hand furniture. Inexpensive, abundant and easy to reinvent, it is a much-loved and valued ingredient of every homespun home.

 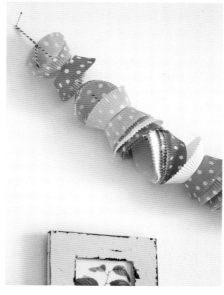 

OPPOSITE Wallpaper can be applied to all sorts of surfaces – not just walls! Here, some vintage floral paper has been used to brighten up the doors of built-in cupboards on a landing.

ABOVE LEFT This beautiful homemade paper bunting incorporates illustrated pages torn from old books.
ABOVE CENTRE Colourful cake cases strung along patterned string

make an eye-catching, inexpensive and very easy to make garland.
ABOVE RIGHT Crocheted doilies have been stuck to a wall as decoration. They look particularly good against a white background.

The 21st-century commitment to recycling goes beyond putting out our empty tin cans and wine bottles for collection. We are adopting the anti-waste message when it comes to decorating our homes, too. Increasingly, we are turning our back on mass-produced furniture made with unsustainable materials and furnishing our rooms with pieces from previous decades.

The beauty of furnishing with second-hand finds is the choice. From cheap and cheerful junk-store finds to classic vintage pieces by celebrated designers, there is a wealth of reusable furniture out there. And the same goes for textiles, accessories, paintings,

wallpapers – the list goes on. You can find it online – eBay is a great place to start – at car boot fairs/yard sales and, if your wallet permits, in antiques shops. Whatever the source, older pieces all have something in common – they have been owned, loved and used, as well as sometimes abused, before! No trees were cut down or dubious methods employed to produce them – or at least not in the last few decades, anyway.

The appeal of reusing furniture goes beyond the ethical, though. There is the simple excitement of shopping at a market or fair – you never know what treasures you might stumble upon.

While chain stores offer a range that you may be familiar with, shopping for older pieces can lead you down some fascinating design routes to some truly unique pieces.

In addition, it also offers a chance to flex your homespun style muscles and get creative. Old pieces, by their very nature, are often worn and tired-looking, but customizing can quickly transform them. When you have only paid a small sum for that cupboard or stool, you have nothing to lose by tinkering with its appearance and sometimes just a coat of bright paint or piece of fabric to cover the seat is all that is needed to give a piece a funky new look.

Don't discount something just because it is broken or frayed either – perhaps you could mend it? If the damage is complex or beyond your skills, it may still be worth spending a little to have it repaired. Or take the easy path – what you can't customize you can always cover up. If you love the bones of a chair but not its upholstery, simply spread a patterned throw over it and you can continue to enjoy its shape, while its appearance is entirely different.

TOP LEFT Old glass bottles make excellent vases and are wide enough to hold an elegant, single stem, as here.

TOP RIGHT A twig suspended from string has been strung with tissue-paper flowers.

ABOVE LEFT An old junk-store china teacup is reborn as a vase, here set into a wall sconce so that it can be hung up.

ABOVE RIGHT Wrapping wire around the neck of a vase allows you to hang it from a hook.

homespun tip Treat your rooms to fresh flowers whenever you can. They bring living colour and vibrancy to any scheme. Pick wild flowers or simply display single stems to keep costs down.

THIS PAGE A second-hand chest of drawers has been reinvented with bright paint, while the door to a cellar has been treated with blackboard paint, transforming it into a giant memo pad ('husk' means remember in Norwegian!).

HUSK !
♡ Garn
♡ Rosa tråd
♡ Bånd
♡ Maling

THIS PAGE Theming artwork gives it cohesion. Here, old floral paintings gain new impact when grouped together. An Anglepoise lamp is a classic design that never goes out of style.

RIGHT This chest of drawers has been customized with a mix of vintage wallpaper and paint, giving each drawer a brave new look. **BELOW** Pretty doilies can be used as coasters, table decorations or taped to walls as artwork. **BOTTOM** It is easy to make your own homespun artwork. Here, fabric offcuts have been stretched across an embroidery ring, and then hung on the wall.

When you are out hunting for second-hand finds, think beyond the obvious original purpose of the piece, too. Wallpaper is just for walls, right? Wrong! Use it to paper drawer fronts or cupboard doors – it's a great way to use up half rolls and offcuts. Finding new uses for old pieces is a chance to give your imagination free rein. Think about an object's colour, pattern or shape first. Focus on whatever draws you to it, then work out how to use it later. It is easy to assign pieces of furniture a new role. A bookcase can be reinvented as a kitchen cabinet. A pretty cup can become a plant holder. Plates can be hung on the walls instead of pictures, and a beautiful scarf can become an even-better cushion cover.

details

textiles

Abundant, inexpensive and guaranteed to make
an impact, textiles are crucial to the homespun
look. Used throughout the house, they can take
any room from plain to personal in an instant.

THIS PAGE Two big cushions covered in a lush green, eye-catching fabric give this scheme a bright focal point. They make a bold contrast with the intricate lacy throw beneath and the detailed patchwork cushion.

textiles marry colour, pattern and softness, making them welcome elements of any homespun room. Incredibly versatile, they can be stitched into a range of roles, or simply thrown over an old seat or sofa to beautifully disguise it.

OPPOSITE A beautiful patchwork bedspread, stitched from fabric remnants, was a wedding present to the owners of this house. It is teamed with large floral print cushions for a dynamic contrast.

ABOVE LEFT Simple muslin curtains have been brightened up with a random pattern of fabric circles, simply stitched in place.
ABOVE CENTRE Look out for textiles on your travels to bring

some strong, ethnic colours into your scheme. Here, Indian shawls and throws are stacked together.
ABOVE RIGHT Retro fabrics make great patchwork cushion covers and crocheted doilies add texture.

Textiles are at the very heart of the homespun home. Combining colour, pattern and tactile appeal all in one, they are an asset to any room. Textiles have the power to transform even the plainest neutral shell into a colourful and welcoming space, and can instantly bring zest and personality to the simplest sofa or dullest of floors. They give you something to snuggle up against, injecting some soft, tactile sensuality into a room. They are flexible, adaptable and very often portable. A throw, cushion, rug or curtain can be embellished, dyed or simply moved to another room, where it will take on a whole new feel.

Tracking down textiles is easy. The more exclusive fabric and soft furnishings stores sell gorgeous materials at a high price, but there is no need to spend a fortune. The homespun house loves vintage finds and buys with a story attached, so look out for second-hand textiles. They are abundant and easy to come by. Markets, eBay and even your grandmother's linen cupboard are all good hunting grounds, whatever your taste.

Remember that when it comes to choosing the right textiles, there are no rules. Have fun mixing fabrics in different shades and styles. Juxtapose tiny flower prints with big, blousy patterns.

homespun tip If your collection of fabric remnants is becoming messy, try colour-coding it. Neatly folded and stacked on open shelves, colour-coded fabric is easy to see, access and organize.

THIS PAGE A built-in bench makes efficient use of space, while also providing useful additional storage. Topped with a long seat pad and scatter cushions, it is a great way to introduce colourful textiles to a white scheme.

Team spots with stripes, and work in lush textures and fun details like pom-poms or sequins, too. Retro cottons in bright, acid shades, scraps of vintage linen softened by time and exquisite embroidery collected in faraway countries can all live happily together. They do not simply belong in the homespun home; they make it what it is.

As well as bringing life to your rooms, textiles have great practical purpose, too, as curtains, cushion covers, upholstery and bedding. Every home relishes these hard-working ingredients. A thick velvet or damask makes a wonderfully draught-proof curtain and helps to conserve heat. Chunky cottons, linens and canvases make durable seat covers, while more delicate fabrics such as silk and muslin are suited to lighter use – on cushion covers, perhaps, or as sheer curtains that diffuse bright sunlight.

If you are confident about your textile choices, then work them onto upholstery or hang patterned

LEFT Rugs are central to homespun chic and introduce welcome texture, pattern and colour at floor level.
ABOVE Mixing textiles creates a vibrant effect. Here, crocheted blankets in a rainbow of shades are piled on top of a beautiful soft cotton quilt with a neat, piped border.

curtains. Alternatively, go for the fail-safe, flexible option and introduce patterned textiles on smaller items. Stick to neutral upholstery on your sofa, then sprinkle over pretty cushions or decorative throws. Opt for plain white bedlinen, but weave in some homespun personality with a patchwork quilt or brilliant bedspread. Just simply folded at the base of your bed, it will still have impact.

In addition to their practical roles, textiles can be purely decorative details in a homespun scheme. From framed fabric swatches that look like beautiful

pictures, to a vintage kimono hung on the wall, their decorative potential is never missed. Even simple swatches of fabric that you have yet to stitch into a cushion cover or tablecloth can look beautiful. Leave them out displayed on a shelf or chair so that you can enjoy their pattern and colour while you figure out their purpose.

If your textile-buying trips have yielded only small remnants, then patchwork designs are an obvious option, making wonderful use of random squares of material. Patchwork cushion covers, bedspreads and throws are key players in the homespun look and can happily employ any kind of fabric. Kitchen cloths, clothing, silk scarves and old linen sacking can all be incorporated into your design. Apply this logic to other textiles, too, finding new roles for them in your home. A mat can make a wall hanging and even the humblest curtain can be cut to make a cover for a tired-out table. When topped off with toughened glass, it will give a junk-store find a fresh new look.

OPPOSITE ABOVE LEFT
Fabrics embroidered with
thick yarns and sequins
feel as good as they look.
OPPOSITE ABOVE RIGHT
Even the buttons on this
chair are adorned with
delicate stitching!
OPPOSITE LEFT A chair
designed by Niki Jones
and boasting embroidered
detailing sits in a quiet
corner of her home.
ABOVE A length of
patterned fabric makes
an ideal room divider.
RIGHT Beautiful shawls
in jewel-bright shades
picked up in India bring
a splash of ethnic beauty
to a homespun scheme.
Their colours stand out
against the darkly painted
wall behind.

furniture & lighting

Teaming form with function, furniture and lighting in a homespun home looks great and works hard. From design classics to second-hand treasures, each piece combines a pinch of practicality with a whole lot of personality.

THIS PAGE These illuminated decorations, originally designed as Christmas lights, are used to brighten and break up a large, blank wall. They create a soft, ambient glow, too, perfect for cosy dinner times. Classic Eames DSW chairs look coolly elegant, while a red highchair provides an invigorating shot of intense colour.
OPPOSITE Tea lights and mini lights provide a warm, atmospheric glow.

furniture & lighting are the hard-working, multitasking staples of any room. They always have a practical role, but must look good, too, so it's worth taking time to hunt down – or create – the perfect piece.

OPPOSITE This handsome wall of shelving, with a matching unit below, once belonged in a kitchen. The owners stripped it back to reveal the wood, and then moved it to their dining space.

ABOVE LEFT A vintage pendant light complete with its original moulded glass shade.
ABOVE CENTRE Rope lighting is a fun and flexible way to create illuminated shapes on walls.

ABOVE RIGHT Even this simple piece of junk-store furniture gains a funky new feel when painted a dazzling swimming-pool turquoise. The large mirror hanging above maximizes the light.

Furniture and lighting are the workhorses of any room. Furniture may be decorative, but it almost always has a function, too. It provides us with storage and somewhere to sit, work or eat. It can be huge in scale, or slim and discreet. It can stand against the wall or take centre stage. Similarly, lighting also has a practical role to play. From the angled desk lamp that lights your workspace to the uplighters that create a soft glow in your living room, it illuminates our interior space, making a life after dusk possible. Beyond that, it creates atmosphere and mood, making it an essential but often overlooked ingredient of any scheme.

There are no strict rights and wrongs when it comes to choosing furniture styles for the homespun home. Anything goes. A good smattering of vintage and second-hand furniture brings a room some much-needed warmth and character, but the sharp lines and grace of a designer piece can also fit in well, introducing some gravitas among all that colour and texture. Similarly, keep your eyes peeled for unique pieces created by modern makers and craftspeople. These will often combine age-old techniques with contemporary forms and innovations, to produce something striking and novel but warm, too.

THIS PAGE The simple lines of the pieces in this room are shown at their best against an all-white background. The wooden table top provides warmth, while accents of green are introduced via the painted chairs and a few decorative accessories.
OPPOSITE A glass-fronted display cabinet shows off favourite pieces. The interior has been painted dark blue to create a striking backdrop.

homespun tip Homespun style places great emphasis on display, so always look out for units and cupboards with glass rather than solid doors. Painting behind the shelves creates a bold backdrop.

Any investment buys you make can be married with junk-store treasures. Second-hand furniture is central to the homespun look. It is both creative and inexpensive to customize a chair seat or paint a wooden table, and it will give your home unique personality.

Don't limit yourself to furniture from one era or in one material. Mix painted wood with stripped wood. Team a squidgy old armchair with a Seventies sideboard. Play with scale, too. A single, dramatic piece of furniture can create more impact than lots of little pieces. Buy what you love. That way you will never tire of it, and can move your furniture from room to room, constantly reinventing your space.

When planning your lighting, remember that it can be divided into three key groups: task, accent and ambient light. Task lighting allows you to do a job well and safely, whether it be chopping vegetables for dinner or reading a novel. Accent lighting focuses on a particular detail, such as books on a shelf or a picture, while ambient lighting is the background light we see by. Ideally, you need a blend of all three in each room.

OPPOSITE This chunky farmhouse dining table flanked by mismatched chairs looks both welcoming and relaxed. A white glass pendant light, hung low over the table, creates an intimate pool of warm light for evening meals, supplemented by flickering candlelight.

ABOVE, LEFT TO RIGHT Hanging strips of fabric from an elegant candelabra gives it a colourful edge; a dramatic shade goes well with a simple, clear glass base; this wall sconce was a market find, spray painted with white gloss and teamed up with a floral lampshade.

BELOW, LEFT TO RIGHT Brightly coloured flex/cord adds a homespun feel to a simple pendant light; small patterns and a narrow trim suit a dainty lampshade such as this one; an inexpensive second-hand lampshade works well with this pretty and unusual wall light.

The greater the number and variety of light sources, the more you can control the light to suit your mood or activities. While it is possible to have only portable light sources such as lamps in your rooms, it is a good idea to have some lighting built in. Well-placed wall lights, a pendant over a dining table or a handsome chandelier will give you a good wash of ambient light. If your budget doesn't run to new lights, customize what you already have. A retro metal pendant will bring homespun style to a boring central fitting, while funky patterned lampshades can brighten up any existing wall sconces.

Then simply weave in some portable light sources, from table and desk lamps to LED rope lighting. Don't forget the oldest light source of all: candlelight. Candles create a relaxing glow that beautifully supplements electrical light.

ABOVE LEFT This workstation has a desk lamp, which provides task lighting for detailed work, and an overhead fitting cloaked in a beautiful capiz shell shade, which creates ambient, background light. Wall-mounted shelves keep the workspace clear and tidy.

THIS PICTURE Rather than a long desk for a workstation, two circular tables do the job here. These are reserved purely for work, thanks to the adjacent wall of built-in shelving, which provides storage for materials, books and equipment.

display

Forget minimalism – homespun style
urges us to celebrate much-loved
pieces by showing them off.
When creatively displayed and
thoughtfully arranged, even
the most everyday objects
will look striking.

THIS PAGE This collage-style wall of images includes children's drawings, photography and postcards. Casually tacking images to a wall like this means they are easy to move and change. **OPPOSITE** A stack of pretty, vintage china gets an extra decorative flourish when it serves as a home to fabric flowers, ribbon and buttons.

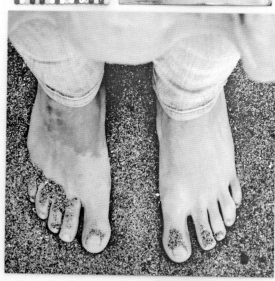

display Personal treasures and quirky, found objects fit happily into a homespun scheme, but think creatively about where and how you display them. Walls are not just for pictures; shelves not just for books, as this section shows…

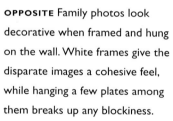

OPPOSITE Family photos look decorative when framed and hung on the wall. White frames give the disparate images a cohesive feel, while hanging a few plates among them breaks up any blockiness.

ABOVE LEFT Fresh flowers from the garden are wound through this crystal chandelier.
ABOVE CENTRE A tiny scrap of vintage embroidery turns into a work of art in its own right when

neatly framed and propped up on a painted chest of drawers.
ABOVE RIGHT Books are arranged here according to the colour of their spines, with a single shelf reserved for trinkets and treasures.

Having furnished and lit your home, it is now time to let rip creatively – the homespun home is all about display. It is the exact opposite of the sleek, modernist house, with possessions stored out of sight and surfaces kept clear. Instead, homespun style is about revelling in exuberant detail and surrounding yourself with beautiful objects and meaningful pieces.

Everyone gathers up items for display as they go through life, from pretty china to old postcards and strings of beads to colourful books. These are not exclusive, expensive items, just everyday treasures. Rather than hiding them away in boxes or behind cupboard doors, the homespun home puts these possessions on display. Necklaces hung from a simple hook look wonderfully decorative, while open shelves allow you to enjoy your objects, even when you are not using them. Save your cupboards for the mundane essentials of daily life: cleaning products in a kitchen, paperwork in a study, DVDs in a living room.

Having your possessions on display is more than just a styling trick, though. It is practical, too, as it makes accessing the things you own much easier. If jewellery is hanging up or cups and bowls are visible, you are more likely to remember each piece and use it.

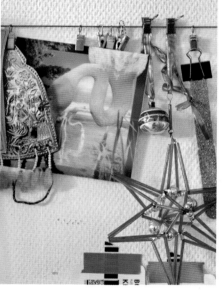

ABOVE LEFT Although this wall looks as though it has been painstakingly adorned with retro postcards and botanical prints casually stuck on with tape, this is actually wallpaper with a pattern printed on. If time or materials are short, it is the perfect way to create a collage effect on walls.

TOP RIGHT The rustic wood of this staircase has postcards pinned to it. The drawing pins/thumbtacks are topped off with buttons, creating a tiny decorative detail.

ABOVE RIGHT A simple wire strung between two nails is the starting point for this varied, ever-changing display. Bulldog clips tied onto the wire grip a mix of baubles, trinkets and pictures.

OPPOSITE Anything can make wall art, from a badge to a photo to tear sheets from magazines and books, as this wall demonstrates beautifully. This vibrant look is flexible, too – you can add to it or move it around.

homespun tip Forget agonizing over the perfect place to hang a picture and adopt the homespun method of sticking a mix of images to your wall, creating an inspiring arrangement that is easy to add to.

No.3

I refuse to let common sense cloud my judgment

KEE
CAL
AND
CAR
ON

LEFT Plates make excellent wall art. Here, a mix of contemporary and vintage china has been hung in a slightly random-seeming display with plates of different shapes and sizes sitting alongside each other. Bold, patterned wallpaper offers a contrasting backdrop.

OPPOSITE ABOVE LEFT Hanging objects from hooks is an easy way to display favourite pieces. A green painted plate rack holds colourful china while metallic-effect cups suspended from hooks add some sparkle.

OPPOSITE ABOVE RIGHT Displayed on open shelves, a colourful collection of china from Arendal Ceramics can be enjoyed even when not in use.

OPPOSITE RIGHT Kitchen shelves stacked with bright china and glassware create a relaxed, homespun feel.

The happy result of this is that your displays will be constantly evolving. A homespun home has an organic quality: the objects within it are enjoyed, touched and used. Consequently, the arrangement of plates in a rack or glasses on a shelf naturally alters as each piece is picked up and put back during the course of daily life.

Buying objects for display is a joy. You do not need to shop armed with measurements or thoughts of practicality, as you might when hunting for furniture. Instead, go with your heart. An object that calls out to you because of its shape or colour is a no-brainer purchase.

Pick it up and find a place for it later. You don't need deep pockets, either. Just wander round a market or fair and see what is on offer. A little money can go a long way.

Think creatively when it comes to choosing what objects you display. Look again at everyday things. When isolated by a glass bell jar or stacked up on a mantelpiece, anything from the humble cotton reel to old paperbacks can look wonderful. Similarly, objects that were once practical, such as old oil cans, printing letter trays or wooden shoe lasts, can looks incredibly decorative when put on display inside your home.

LEFT Handmade fabric flowers are scattered over this stencilled table. **BELOW LEFT** A simple shelf unit is the perfect place to display favourite pieces. Each object is loosely colour-matched with the wallpaper behind, for a harmonious look. **BELOW RIGHT** Standing a bell jar over any pretty objects, even simple cotton reels, gives them extra decorative impact.

Display on your walls can be relaxed. Forget any notions of symmetry and have fun with how you hang art. Framed black and white photos look great against riotously bright wallpaper. Pepper your wall with plates picked up in junk stores or just pin or tape postcards to a wall. Flexibility is key.

If you are worried that this relaxed approach could descend into a design free-for-all, bring some gentle order to your displays by colour-coordinating them. Arrange books on a shelf according to the colour of their spine, or loosely theme a shelf of crockery by shade. If you like the idea of hanging lots of small pictures rather than one or two large ones, give them some cohesion by choosing frames in the same shade. This way, the homespun look remains informal, but also well thought through and balanced.

THIS PAGE Black and white family photographs in austere dark frames make a witty contrast to the retro pink wallpaper and hot orange chair in this workspace. The pictures have been hung in a relaxed fashion, roughly creating a circular shape, to complement the wallpaper's circular motif.

spaces

When it comes to relaxing, the living room reigns supreme. Its purpose today is less formal gathering place, more comfort zone. This is the one public room dedicated to downtime, and soft textures, warm colours and a sink-into sofa will create a friendly feel.

relaxed living

Homespun style places great emphasis on easy-going comfort – it is at the heart of the look – but, as one of the most sociable places in the house, your living room must work hard, too. So it is essential to get the foundations right. Take time to work out exactly how the space should function for you and your family. Will your living room be a relaxing snug, a versatile entertaining space or the family hang-out? You will need to work in the appropriate flooring, storage and furniture to suit each role. In a family-biased room, that might mean squashy sofas with washable covers and a hard-wearing floor. In a more grown-up space, it might mean a shapely corner sofa, coffee table and lots of tactile rugs.

FAR LEFT Built-in shelving is an asset in even the smallest living space, combining storage and room for display, too.
ABOVE LEFT A corner sofa dotted with bright cushions creates a sociable space with a coffee table, not a TV, its focus. White floors and walls keep the look fresh.
ABOVE Books don't have to be stored on shelves. A tower of them looks colourful and decorative.

THIS PAGE This living space breaks the rule that says stick to neutral upholstery on furniture and add pattern with cushions. Here, a sofa covered in boldly patterned fabric is the focal point. Walls are strongly coloured but plain, allowing the floral design to sing out.

It is helpful to look at your room bare – or at least imagine it without any furnishings – to assess its best features. Every living space has its own personality. There may be a striking fireplace or large windows, for example. The light may fall in an interesting way and this may influence the choices you make. There may be original features, such as mouldings, dado/chair rails or handsome panelling, all worth drawing attention to.

On the other hand, a close look at your living space may reveal a lack of interesting features. Don't worry – you can easily work in some personality using reclaimed pieces. Visit a salvage yard for a striking period door, fire surround or salvaged wooden flooring to add instant warmth and homespun character.

When considering your walls, remember that most homespun living rooms carry colour and pattern on soft furnishings, textiles and painted furniture, preferring neutral walls as a backdrop. This makes decorating simple and is kind to your wallet, too. Forget colours from expensive paint ranges, when a basic pot of white will do. In a small room, steer clear of pure brilliant white, though.

THIS PAGE & OPPOSITE Wooden panelled walls in this Scandinavian home add welcome detail, despite being simply painted white. Against this fresh backdrop coloured furniture stands out, but here the wooden pieces have been painted not in eye-popping shades but calming pink, peach and apple green. The sofa, by contrast, is a modern, neutral piece that helps anchor the scheme and is brightened with cushions. Artwork is casually arranged, some along a shelf, which allows the pictures to be moved around easily.

THIS PAGE Armchairs upholstered in a mix of eye-catching fabrics give this otherwise neutral living space bags of homespun style. Floorboards are left untreated, while a sisal rug adds natural texture.

THIS PAGE The tradition of creating storage in the area under the stairs is tweaked here. Rather than a built-in cupboard, open shelves provide room for displaying china, and all the floor space that would usually be hidden is available for a comfy armchair.

LEFT The homespun look loves colour and even when used quite minimally it can have a huge impact. This snowy white scheme is punctuated only by cut flowers and two simple paintings. Tongue-and-groove wall panels add some welcome detail within this pale palette.
OPPOSITE Pops of mustardy yellow create focal points in this corner, while bleached wooden flooring bucks the all-white trend without creating a harsh contrast. Fresh flowers, with their deep green leaves, bring the space alive.

It contains optical brighteners and can over-reflect, creating an uncomfortable, dazzling effect. Then have fun with colour on a small scale. Create a feature wall with a strong shade, or add some drama by painting a door. Use a contrasting bright on the frame for an extra flash of colour.

The floor is the second-largest surface in any room after the walls, so it needs careful thought, too. While living rooms are about relaxing, they also experience a fair amount of traffic, so a practical surface teamed with soft rugs that are kind to bare feet works well. Solid wood flooring is a great option. It is sturdy underfoot and can be painted to suit the room. Pale boards will instantly brighten a dark room, bouncing natural light upwards, while old boards, hidden under carpet for years, can be sanded down and sealed for a fresh new look. If you are laying a new floor, choose thin boards to make a narrow space appear wider and wide boards to balance the proportions of a large room.

Natural light is a key ingredient of the homespun look, so keep window treatments simple. Roller blinds or unfussy sheers allow light to flood in. If you fancy a flash of colour at your window, hang simple banners made with colourful fabric. Silk works well; try leaving it unlined for a breezy, billowy feel. In darker rooms, hang a large mirror, too, to dramatically boost light levels.

With the bones in place, you can think about the ingredients of your living space. Does there need to be a TV in here? Would you like to include a desk for working, or is this purely a relaxing zone? Will it be a simple space, or will it multitask as a home for books and possessions, too?

Many homespun living spaces focus purely on relaxation. They are somewhere to read, chat or spend time on a hobby. So the TV is banished to another room and furniture is positioned with sociability in mind. The focus of the room becomes a coffee table or a fireplace instead. Be aware that such configurations, particularly in open-plan rooms, may mean your furniture is viewed from all angles. Make sure it looks as good from the back as from the front!

RIGHT Sofas can be a huge investment, but the homespun style shows how even the simplest piece can become something beautiful without the need to spend a fortune. Here, lush green fabric is used to cover a no-frills sofa, while a second-hand cane chair is brightened up with throws and a cushion. Simple, painted wooden furniture completes the relaxed, colourful look.

THIS PAGE A puffy quilt is used to brighten and soften this white sofa. Stools painted in similar tones tie in with the patterned fabrics and create a casual place to perch, while simple artwork in black and white and an imposing mirror prevents the look from feeling too cute.

Although homespun style revels in its eclectic mix of furniture, it also includes some built-in pieces. Built-in cupboards, shelves and benches with storage beneath make great use of alcoves and awkward corners that would otherwise have no purpose. Built-in shelves also provide essential space for displaying treasures or books; pieces that remind you of who you are and what you love, to create a cosy, homespun feel.

When it comes to freestanding pieces, one key ingredient of the homespun living space is a sofa. If you are buying a new sofa and it is destined to see a lot of action, choose one with a strong frame. Hard wood or metal frames are toughest. Easy-to-clean covers are also important. Loose slipcovers are washable – perfect for family life – and once

ABOVE The simple recipe of neutral upholstery and colourful cushions works brilliantly here. Shelves that store books and magazines with their covers facing out add interest to a plain wall. LEFT A large cupboard provides storage for living-space essentials such as DVDs, leaving the room uncluttered.

laundered, put them back on while damp, as they will shrink to fit like a pair of jeans. A fabric with a tight weave is also practical, as crumbs and pet hair will brush off more easily. If space is limited, go for a compact sofa on legs – being able to see around and beneath the piece gives the illusion of more space.

Whether your sofa is brand new, second-hand or just a long-standing member of your household, a simple throw or blanket spread over it is a homespun staple. It will protect the sofa from marks and stains, hide signs of wear and introduce colour

and pattern to your scheme. A sofa in a colour that contrasts with the walls and floor will never fade into the background, and again, throws and blankets are all you need to create this stand-out look. Then just add bright cushions in a mishmash of patterns for extra cosy appeal.

Underfoot, rugs are essential. From sheepskins to vibrant ethnic weaves, they bring personality and comfort to your floor. The good news is that they need not be expensive. Second-hand rugs can look

wonderful and a small amount of wear only adds to their personality. Don't be put off by marks. If your rug is professionally cleaned (or even dry cleaned, if it is small), it will look beautiful again. Rugs not only add comfort, colour and pattern, they help soundproof your space, too – ideal if you live in an apartment. They can also delineate zones, which is useful in an open-plan space. Try arranging sofas around a low table with a rug beneath it to define a relaxation area.

THIS PAGE Positioned close to a huge window, this bench makes an inviting place to sit and read or have coffee. The large-scale floral pattern on the rug is picked up but balanced by smaller, more intricate patterns on the cushions.

OPPOSITE FAR LEFT & BELOW LEFT Brightly coloured textiles give this top-floor living space masses of vibrancy. Colour is also supplied via the artwork and its frames, painted a hot, neon pink shade.

OPPOSITE LEFT Cane furniture is lightweight, pretty and inexpensive. Here, it is scattered with pretty cushions in soft pinks and greens, and framed by an open window. Garlands and mini lights add further touches of colour, draped over a mirror and hung from the ceiling.

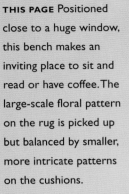

OPPOSITE This partially sheltered balcony has been transformed into a cosy living space, with a homemade day bed, potted plants and plenty of cushions.

ABOVE & BELOW RIGHT This living space maximizes the light from the French windows with white on walls and flooring, and sheer curtains wittily hung from a branch rather than a pole. Cushions in retro floral fabric lend a further touch of humour.

TOP RIGHT Favourite pieces displayed in a compartmentalized tray.

THIS PAGE Vintage Tolix chairs with distressed paintwork set the relaxed tone of this cooking and eating space. A window onto a neighbouring room is given real character with a lemon-yellow-painted frame, and this fresh shade is found on vases and china, too, creating cohesion.

Cooking and eating spaces, now so often the same room in a house, see much of family life. They are somewhere to work, play, cook, eat, socialize or just enjoy a cup of coffee. So a vibrant homespun scheme that blends practicality with comfort is perfect.

cooking & eating

Even just a few decades ago, we ate and cooked in two very different places in the home. Food was prepared in the kitchen, often at the back of the house, while eating took place in a separate dining room. Today, we like to cook and eat in the same open-plan space, which, with homespun style, can become a busy but gorgeous hub.

Cooking and eating spaces have so much to recommend them. They are functional and convenient: the kettle is to hand for coffee while you browse the paper; the table is handily close when you are serving meals. They are also highly sociable spaces. You can make dinner while your children do their homework or friends chat to you.

LEFT AND ABOVE The complete opposite of a minimalist kitchen, a homespun cooking space derives its sense of style from having everything out on display. Colourful open shelves make a handsome home for a collection of pretty china, while utensils create more impact when casually crammed into an old can or hanging from a simple rack, making them easy to access, too.

ABOVE Colourful china is a favourite of the homespun look. Here, mismatched pieces that share a pretty, floral theme work wonderfully together.

ABOVE CENTRE These chillies look too colourful to be hidden in a cupboard and clash brilliantly with the pink bowl. The cushion is covered in Indian fabric with characteristic visible stitching.

ABOVE RIGHT Coloured glasses pack a homespun punch.

BELOW Even the most practical of cooking and eating space essentials can be creatively displayed. Here, stacks of colourful tea/dish towels, place mats and melamine cutlery look fantastic on an open shelf.

BELOW RIGHT It is easy to pick up retro storage jars at markets and they are incredibly useful, too. This canister has been personalized with a sweet stuck-on message.

THIS PAGE The table in this welcoming eating space is lit by a pendant light, fitted with a homemade papier-mâché shade. The plastic matting on the floor is colourful, extremely hard-wearing and helps to zone the space, too.

Everyone can be together, to share and help with preparing food or setting the table, for that friendly, relaxed feel that is so central to homespun style.

An open-plan cooking and eating area also makes more efficient use of the available space than individual rooms – ideal in smaller properties. Don't let the size of your kitchen deter you from using it as an eating space. Good design and thoughtful storage can create enough space for a small table and chairs, or consider having bench seating built in, which is space-saving and can be designed to contain vital storage, too. In bigger rooms, let your imagination run free. With the right square footage, anything can go into a cooking and eating space, from high-tech appliances to sofas and bookcases.

When it comes to furnishing your cooking and eating space, homespun style takes a loose, organic approach to even this highly functional room. If you are starting from scratch, resist the temptation to

OPPOSITE This relaxed eating space is all about florals, with its patterned fabrics, retro wallpaper and vintage flower paintings. The old table is covered with a practical floral oilcloth, too.
LEFT Open shelves allow you to see and enjoy pieces that are not in use.
ABOVE The blue walls of this eating space on a covered terrace, create a rich background for mismatched cushions.

install banks of built-in cupboards. Wall-hung units in particular can crowd out the space – a design faux pas in a small kitchen. Instead, try teaming built-in floor cupboards with pieces of freestanding furniture. Dressers, glass-fronted cabinets, sideboards and even old wardrobes, sourced at markets or antique fairs, can hold a huge amount of kitchen equipment, while a large table can double up as a work surface. Alternatively, track down furniture from the Forties and Fifties. Kitchens in this period typically included a mix of built-in and freestanding pieces, and you can find beautiful period cupboards in second-hand stores.

LEFT While modern kitchens are often focused on functionality, the homespun cooking space aims to be decorative, too. Here, a vintage glass-fronted cabinet and painted shelf look so much more characterful than a conventional kitchen cupboard or worktop. **OPPOSITE** Furniture that has seen a bit of life, like this slightly chipped table and chairs, brings warmth to an eating space. Peg rails are another useful addition, providing space for hanging pretty bags.

RIGHT, FAR RIGHT & ABOVE RIGHT This pretty cooking space has a colourful gingham curtain as an alternative to a cupboard door. The owner has decorated the fridge using a green circular stamp, while inexpensive white tiles are given some welcome personality with cute animal-motif designs dotted among them.

If your existing kitchen cabinetry is sound but lacking in personality, there is much you can do. Consider refreshing your units with new doors – there are many specialists supplying made-to-measure doors in a range of colours and finishes – or paint the old doors yourself. Even replacing boring handles with pretty knobs will lift the look of a plain cabinet. Stringing a homemade fabric panel in front of shelves or appliances is another budget makeover and a great way to introduce colour and pattern, too. If your splashback lacks charm, replace it with reclaimed tiles or some funky wallpaper, sealed behind Perspex or glass. Then work in some open shelving, to show off your favourite pieces while keeping them conveniently to hand.

The disadvantage of a totally open-plan space is that you are eating or socializing right next to your oven or sink, so think carefully about where you position your table and, if space allows, create a simple waist-height divide between your cooking and eating areas with a freestanding shelving unit. Source your table, chairs and other furniture at popular homespun hunting grounds such as markets or fairs. A lick of paint can restore woodwork, while a practical oilcloth will conceal marks on a table top.

Practical ingredients like appliances need careful consideration. White goods are kitchen essentials, but can look unappealingly workmanlike, so, if possible, hide them within built-in units or behind a funky curtain. Alternatively, if your budget allows, invest in retro-style appliances, such as Smeg's FAB range, with its soft lines and cheerful colours. Remember to work in lighting that is both functional and atmospheric, too. Install task lighting in food preparation areas and softer downlighting for meal times. Positioning pendant lights over a table is a stock homespun-style look, helping to zone the area and create a cosy glow ideal for dining.

In an open-plan area like a cooking and eating space, flooring is abundantly visible. If you want to make the space feel bigger, use the same flooring throughout. Alternatively, you could zone the space by choosing two or three different materials or colours to distinguish between cooking and eating areas. Laying washable rugs or mats to define these areas is also effective, as is simply painting floorboards a different shade to show where one section ends and the other begins.

ABOVE & FAR RIGHT Splashes of red and green on the glassware in this pretty white cabinet add some colour to the sparkly display. Flea markets and fairs are a great hunting ground for vintage glass like this. **RIGHT** Coloured tiles and shelves brimming with pretty china and cookware give this wall easy-going charm.

THIS PAGE Mixing vintage and modern is a favourite homespun trick. Here, a contemporary metal-framed table is flanked by homely, painted wooden furniture. Elegant glass pendant lights hang over the table, creating a soft glow for dining, while the window is curtain-free, to maximize daylight.

THIS PAGE This simple scheme of white and wood would suit any eating space and is wonderfully easy to pull off. Colour has been introduced with fresh flowers, and clutter is avoided thanks to storage along one wall.

LEFT This storage unit has sliding doors, so the china and glassware housed inside can be on display or hidden away, as desired.

ABOVE LEFT Pretty magnets make a colourful display on this fridge. Pom-poms and crocheted designs hold a child's painting in place.

ABOVE This traditional cupboard once belonged in a kitchen. Now restored, it is a handsome and practical addition to this eating space, storing china and glassware conveniently to hand. Its simple combination of stripped and white-painted wood is picked up by the table and painted chairs.

THIS PICTURE & LEFT This colourful cooking space uses wallpaper swatches as a splashback, giving a homespun edge to the industrial-style units. Colour is added in surprising ways, too — on the retro-style fridge and the Ikea chairs. A patchwork tablecloth completes the look.

Forget coordinated china or matching cutlery, too: the homespun look revels in a cheerful diversity of colour, form and pattern. This makes kitting out your cooking and eating space simple. After all, when your crockery is mismatched already, it is easy to add to, and when the only thing your furniture has in common is bright paintwork, any new piece, whatever its shape, can be painted to fit in.

Despite the homespun preference for open shelving and display, some pieces of kitchen kit will need to be stored away. Gadgets such as electric mixers, oversize pans and beaten-up baking sheets won't add to the aesthetic appeal of your room, so stash them in cupboards or baskets. Similarly, many foodstuffs offer little in the way of good looks. It is almost impossible to make a bag of potatoes look stylish, so keep

THIS PAGE An elegant eating space is taken from formal to relaxed thanks to colourful seat pads and a sprinkling of cushions along the wooden bench. Even the candelabra has been given a homespun makeover, with strips of vintage fabric strung from it, creating a visual link between the seating and the space above.

LEFT & FAR LEFT This simple kitchen has a cosy corner for eating, too. White units, worktops and a table are cheered up with pretty bunting, hand cloths and a table runner. An old-fashioned plate rack doubles as a bookcase, too.
BELOW This smart, modern kitchen has its slightly austere feel rounded off with simple homespun touches. Bunting, colourful china on open shelving and a bright rug transform and soften the dark wood and white combination.

ingredients like this behind closed doors. Other staples, such as pasta, rice and sugar, can earn a place on an open shelf when contained in attractive storage jars, second-hand Kilner jars or colourful metal canisters picked up at markets.

Love of colour and form is central to homespun style but so, too, is balance, and achieving a balance between decorative and functional is important. Objects openly displayed bring essential personality, yet too many can make the space look messy and distracting. Be selective about what you display. Cutlery doesn't need to be stored in drawers. Keep it accessible on open shelves, stacked in jars or old tin cans. Even a row of honest, hard-working utensils – ladles, slotted spoons, palette knives – can look decorative when hung from butcher's hooks. Put up peg rails, hooks and plate racks, too, all of which offer space for hanging and displaying anything from pretty tea towels/dish cloths to patterned china. Then store the boring pieces of kitchen kit out of sight for that perfect blend of decoration and calm, uncluttered space.

LEFT Originally, this shelf was probably designed for use in a hallway, but it works really well in this kitchen. Hooks are handy additions, providing space to hang all kinds of kitchen kit.

RIGHT A chic kitchen with a high-gloss finish and black rubber flooring is given a blast of quirky personality thanks to a wallpaper splashback, sealed behind glass. Bright china introduces further colour to the scheme.

FAR LEFT & LEFT Chunky farmhouse-style units are teamed with a freestanding Forties kitchen cupboard in this cosy cooking and eating space. Soft turquoise walls look fresh and cheerful, and the colour is picked up by the patterned china. An awkward alcove has been put to good use and is now home to three useful shelves.

THIS PAGE Laying a rug underneath a dining table is a simple way to zone the eating space in an open-plan, multitasking room. This simple stripe design also brings some focus to a pale scheme. Wooden chairs painted in bold shades and colourful candlesticks help to punctuate the white still more, while fresh blooms bring some natural colour. Cut flowers wilt after about a week, so here, a potted geranium makes a wonderful alternative, providing beautiful, living colour month after month.

Unlike the more sociable rooms of a home, the bedroom and bathroom are personal, private spaces. Of course they are used for noisy children's bathtimes, a hurried shower or speedy dressing before work, but they are also intimate rooms where we head for quiet relaxation. In the homespun home, these areas blend practicality with unique, personal style. They use colour, pattern and revamped vintage pieces to create a look that is welcoming, original and just a little bit quirky.

sleeping & bathing

Bedrooms can be a bit of an afterthought. It is partly because they are private spaces where few people venture, and also because we mainly use them at the beginning and end of the day; for dressing in the morning and sleeping at night. Yet the homespun look makes it easy to inject some personality into the bedroom, so it becomes a room you dip in and out of throughout the day.

Unlike busy, multitasking kitchens, bedrooms are primarily about rest and relaxation. Sleep experts recommend creating as calm an atmosphere as possible, to guarantee restful sleep. So that means no television or computer in the bedroom, plenty of soft, tactile materials and good, thick curtains to

LEFT An original Seventies bedspread in grass-green tones looks great against the white walls of this bedroom. It is topped off with cushions stitched from retro fabric offcuts, for a clashing and characterful homespun feel.
ABOVE This beautiful jacket, worn by its owner at her wedding, is hung up on display in the bedroom as a reminder of that special day.

THIS PAGE The wall behind this headboard has been pasted with squares of retro wallpaper to beautifully frame the bed. Patchwork cushions on the bed continue the theme. Clip-on lights attached to the headboard saves space on the bedside tables.

RIGHT This bedroom has an incredibly simple scheme of beige and turquoise, but it looks wonderfully inviting. Your eye is drawn from the blue on the bedding to the retro anglepoise lamp and up to the seaside painting, with a bright pink cushion at the heart of the look – literally!

OPPOSITE A beautiful carved wooden bed makes a bold statement in this small attic room, but painting it white helps it slot in. A brave mix of ethnic, floral and retro fabrics bring homely style, with the yellow picked up in the lampshades.

keep out the early morning sunlight. A roller blind in blackout fabric will also do the trick, and you can hang a pair of decorative curtains in front if desired. Work in bright colours on bedding or with a single wall of wallpaper, but balance this with neutral flooring or white walls, to prevent the scheme becoming too busy. You don't want to be distracted by a riot of pattern and clashing shades when you are trying to drift off to sleep.

To create a tranquil mood, good storage is essential. A good-sized wardrobe teamed with a chunky chest of drawers will do. Excess or out-of-season clothes can be stored in boxes under the bed or on top of a wardrobe. Hunt around flea markets or fairs for vintage furniture that will add a dash of homespun personality to the bedroom without breaking the bank. Apply the same principles of recycling and restoring as you have elsewhere, too.

TOP LEFT These clothes look striking hung against a wall in this bedroom and can be moved or replaced with ease. Hangers sporting crocheted covers add a splash more decoration.

TOP RIGHT Adding a sofa to your sleeping space turns it into somewhere to read or relax in rather than simply sleep in. This vintage piece stands on wooden legs, so it doesn't appear too bulky.

BOTTOM LEFT Jewellery stored casually in a bowl looks pretty and is easily accessible, too.

BOTTOM RIGHT An intricate doily has been simply taped to this wall as a decoration, alongside photos and drawings.

OPPOSITE Walls in soft green create a pale background of mellow colour, complemented by simple bedding in aqua tones and a headboard covered in blue fabric.

FAR LEFT Cushions gain impact with a stitched-on message. **LEFT** A built-in window seat, simply made from a piece of wood topped with cushions, is the perfect place to read or relax. **BELOW & OPPOSITE** There is a clever mix of hard, clean lines and rustic touches in this sleeping space. A bank of drawer units supply most of the storage, while a tree branch suspended from the ceiling creates space to display favourite clothes and accessories. The pendant light and mirror introduce some sparkle, while colour comes via a purple throw.

An old wooden chest of drawers can easily be painted, and if you can't stretch to a French armoire, pick up an inexpensive cupboard and customize it with wallpaper.

The bed is the dominant feature in any bedroom, so lavish some attention on it. You don't really see your bed when you are in it – certainly not once you are asleep! – so make it shine when not in use. Choose neutral linen that can be layered with colourful throws and blankets, or tweak convention and ditch the matching set in favour of sheets, duvet covers and pillowcases in contrasting colours and patterns. This conjures up instant homespun appeal, and means making up the bed is easy – just grab any bedding to hand and see what combinations you create. Then pile on snug, homespun touches: patchwork quilts, a colourful bedspread, an old eiderdown inherited from granny and, of course, mountains of cushions.

The bedroom doesn't experience much traffic and is one room we often walk barefoot in, so have fun with tactile flooring. Deep-pile rugs and luxurious, super-soft

sheepskins work particularly well here and increase the feeling of cosiness. If space allows, an armchair is a wonderful addition, too, and will encourage you to use your bedroom during the day, as a place to read, sew or relax. In a small room, a built-in window seat makes good use of the space, or arrange cushions or thick blankets on top of a sturdy chest that can serve as storage and seating in one.

Homespun style loves display, but keep only decorative treasures on show, stashing away your cosmetics bottles, socks and hairdryer. Think creatively about those pieces often stored out of sight, too – could they be put on display? A simple peg rail allows you to hang up gorgeous handbags, a delicate blouse or pretty scarves, so you can enjoy them when not in use. Hooks are great homes for necklaces and bangles, too, with an added practical bonus – if you can see and easily reach your jewellery, you are much more likely to wear it.

Just like kitchens, homespun bathing spaces are not crammed with the latest technology. There is no need to rip out what already exists to create the homespun look. Work with what is there. A plain white suite is the perfect foil for some hearty colour. Painting walls or window frames in a fresh shade is easy and inexpensive, or go for something permanent and create a twinkling splashback or shower surround using mosaics or coloured tiles.

TOP LEFT Decorative balls piled into a bowl make a beautiful feature. **LEFT & OPPOSITE** Coloured walls, cushions and bedding work well together here. The trick is to use a muted tone on walls, against which pops of magenta, gold, black and white stand out. Layering bedding and cushions creates a luxurious feel.

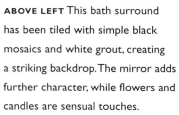

ABOVE LEFT This bath surround has been tiled with simple black mosaics and white grout, creating a striking backdrop. The mirror adds further character, while flowers and candles are sensual touches.

ABOVE CENTRE Paper baubles hung in a window add playful colour to a room.
ABOVE RIGHT Vintage tiles are easy to come by and bring masses of character to any bathing space.

OPPOSITE All kinds of materials make it onto the walls of a homespun home! Here, a collection of vintage tiles, hung in a roughly symmetrical arrangement, makes a striking and unusual artwork.

Bathrooms have a clear practical purpose, but these days we want more from them – they must also function as a personal sanctuary. It is easy to meet both these needs with homespun style. Choose from a vast array of waterproof, hard-wearing flooring that is practical but decorative, from simple vinyl to ceramic tiles or painted floorboards. Wall tiles and mosaics also come in hundreds of different designs and shades, and if your budget is tight, simply dot in a few decorative tiles among a wall of inexpensive plain white ones. A mirror is another essential item, but think beyond the plain mirrored cabinets peddled by bathroom showrooms and shop on eBay or at markets for something more dramatic, complete with an ornate frame.

Finally, think about display. As in the bedroom, you will need some closed storage for all those unsightly essentials, from bottles of mouthwash to shaving foam. Forget boring bathroom cabinets and consider using a vintage chest of drawers or an old console instead. A large piece could also be adapted to support a sink, for a really innovative look. Then display only those bathroom ingredients that are pleasing to the eye. Colourful towels folded on open shelves add a shot of vibrancy, as do pretty washbags and brushes hung from hooks.

As always, homespun style urges us to think outside the box. Could any everyday bathroom essentials be displayed, too? Small bars of soap look pretty tossed into glass storage jars, while bubble bath and liquid soap can be decanted into pots and bottles. Then give the space those finishing touches that will guarantee it becomes more sanctuary than practical washroom. Add scented candles or tea lights in beautiful holders, spread colourful, toe-tickling bath mats and rugs and treat the room to fresh flowers. Finally, fit a lock on the door! And relax...

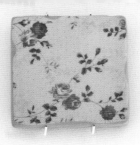

THIS PAGE Bathrooms need storage as much as any room and here a vintage sideboard provides space for bottles and bits. It has been painted white with wallpaper pasted to its doors, for a softer look. The freestanding bathtub is a modern version of the classic slipper bath.

LEFT Second-hand furniture crops up all over the homespun home. In this bathroom, an old cabinet has been used as a washstand. Painted blue, it stands out beautifully against the black and white flooring.

TOP LEFT Even a novice with a needle and thread can run up one of these cute washbags. Stitched from a patchwork of retro fabrics, they look extra colourful hung together from this cupboard door.

ABOVE A modern sink looks really funky teamed with a splashback of retro wallpaper and an antique mirror. A wire shelf with peg rail on the wall provides somewhere to hang colourful towels and bags.

THIS PAGE Homespun touches work well in a child's room, where comfort and cosiness are key. Cushions shaped like animals and layers of bedding make this bed a comfy place to curl up at any time of day. To avoid overstimulating a child and ensure peaceful bedtimes, walls are painted a muted beige.

No other room needs to change and develop as much as a child's room, because no other family members change as much as the children. From baby to toddler to confident school-age child, your offspring's needs and tastes are constantly evolving, so his or her bedroom must keep up. Use some classic homespun touches to anchor this ever-changing room and you can't fail. Splashes of colour, cheerful decoration, painted furniture and squishy cushions will delight any child, at any age or stage.

children's rooms

A nursery can be as simple or as decorative as you choose, but it is your choice! A baby is too busy learning to sit up, walk and talk to care much about interior design. He or she doesn't need much furniture, so the space can contain as little as a cot/crib, a chest of drawers and a comfortable chair for feeds, cuddles and bedtime stories. The nursery's main role is to provide a comfy, calm environment for a baby to sleep in, so subtle lighting, soft surfaces and light-excluding window treatments are all vital. To these foundations, you can add homespun touches. Colourful artworks, pretty bunting, jolly mobiles or bright lampshades that cast a pleasing glow will create a cheerful atmosphere and give your baby something to gaze at from their cot/crib.

LEFT Soft toys hand-stitched from scraps of patterned fabric and adorned with old buttons look delightfully quirky and unique.

ABOVE Clothes for little girls are often incredibly colourful and cute. To enjoy all that pattern and prettiness, here dresses have been hung on a rail from coloured hangers in a rainbow of bright shades. The vintage pink floral wallpaper behind adds to the cheerful mix.

THIS PAGE & OPPOSITE Wallpaper has been used in all kinds of innovative ways in this colourful child's room. A collage tree has been pasted to one wall, with homemade, wallpapered bird boxes attached to the branches. Each partition of a large shelving unit is backed with colourful wallpaper, too, creating a patchwork of designs, while an old cupboard has been painted yellow and its doors lined with vintage rose paper.

BIBI'S
GENERAL
STORE

As your baby reaches toddler stage and begins to play with toys, more storage becomes necessary. A mix of low-level storage that is easily accessible to little ones and high shelving for displaying pretty pieces works well. Baskets, plastic crates and wooden storage boxes are fantastic staples that make tidying easy – just sweep everything into them. If space is tight, find containers that can slide under the cot/crib or bed, or stack on shelves. As you introduce more furniture, keep an eye on safety. Any storage must be securely fastened to the wall and objects chosen for looks rather than purpose should be displayed out of reach.

When sourcing furniture for your child's room, think beyond the obvious mass-produced pieces. Most modern furniture retailers carry a children's range, but you might be surprised to discover how much vintage children's furniture is

OPPOSITE TOP & BOTTOM A tree cut from vintage animal-print wallpaper grows up the wall of this child's room, complete with leaves, knitted and felted owls and homemade bird boxes! A mezzanine bed is reached by a flight of pink stairs, leaving room below for a desk – ideal in an older child's room, in which space to do homework is a priority. **BELOW** Mini lights strung from a bedstead look pretty and their soft glow can serve as a night-light, too. Forget expensive wall stickers – here, the owner has cut out bird shapes from wallpaper and pasted them to the wall. **RIGHT** Painting an old wardrobe then pasting its doors with a mix of wallpaper designs instantly transforms it.

out there. Some of it, like small chairs and wooden desks with flip-top lids, would have been used in schools. Much of it is inexpensive, too – ideal if your child will outgrow it in a few years' time.

Other vintage pieces were built specifically for a child's room. Look out for wooden or iron children's bed frames. New wooden base slats and a fresh mattress will turn them into a characterful, comfortable place to sleep. Wooden child-size chairs and benches are also easy to come by and can be easily renovated with a coat of paint. Think creatively. Furniture designed for other spaces may also serve well in a child's room. A low coffee table can make a workstation or play table for a train set or Lego. A metal or wooden filing cabinet can be sturdy, generous storage for toys and games. Remember the power of a homespun revamp, too! Disguise the dark wood or dated shape of a junk-store wardrobe by pasting wallpaper to its front.

THIS PAGE Children love colour, but to avoid overstimulation, it is a good idea to introduce it on only one wall. Here, a striking design of birds and flowers looks gorgeous, and the pinks in it beautifully match the bedspread and cushions. The alcove, filled with treasures picked up on travels, is deliberately left white, so each piece stands out.

ABOVE This vintage desk has shelves built in, so favourite pieces can be displayed. It has been painted in bubble-gum shades and teamed with a yellow box and pink-painted chair, proving that bold combinations can look wonderful when the backdrop remains white.

ABOVE RIGHT Another tree collage, this time flanked by retro horse prints. The natural theme is picked up by the lampshade, which looks like a giant flower head.

RIGHT Retro prints are bright and fun – perfect for a child's room – while a desk chair painted in soft green serves as a bedside table.

The walls, floor and lighting in a child's room must marry practicality with fun. Children spend a great deal of time on the floor, so think carefully about this area. Soft carpet or fluffy rugs are kind to knees, but can be tricky to lay train track over! Similarly, jigsaw puzzles or Lego pieces may get lost in deep pile. A combination of wooden or vinyl flooring and rugs with a short, close weave works well. Rugs are also a great way to introduce colour and pattern – just keep the floor beneath neutral to avoid overkill. To this base add squishy beanbags or floor cushions in bright, cheerful fabrics, where children can lounge, read or listen to a story.

ABOVE RIGHT This narrow space is just wide enough for a cot/crib. Brightly painted in cherry red, it makes a mini style statement, while bunting and paper lampshades above provide shapes and colour for baby to enjoy while lying in it.

RIGHT The panelled door of this vintage wardrobe lends itself to customization – a strip of wallpaper fits it neatly.

THIS PAGE & OPPOSITE
ABOVE LEFT This room beautifully demonstrates how vintage finds can look just as much at home in a child's sleeping space as in a living or dining space. This shapely armchair is big enough for both parent and child to sit comfortably for a bedtime story, while a retro sideboard offers excellent toy and book storage. Against the white backdrop, even a child's toy stove looks cute, flanked by hooks to hold real utensils.

THIS PAGE This small-scale furniture caters stylishly for children and gives them somewhere to congregate when the adults are eating round the big table. Vintage children's furniture crops up regularly at markets and fairs, so it is easy to come by and often inexpensive.

Lighting needs consideration. Children use their bedrooms for a range of activities, from a sedate jigsaw to a raucous pillow fight. They also come to their bedroom to do potentially eyestraining work such as reading, homework or colouring. Strong background light is important. Wall-mounted uplighters and central ceiling lights with colourful shades are all helpful, but boost these with task lighting, such as a desk lamp or clip-on reading light that provides strong, directional light. Shop in fairs or on eBay for a retro anglepoise lamp or funky pendant that teams practicality with a homespun vibe.

The lighting in a child's bedroom must do more than cater for activity. It must also encourage sleep. Many children struggle to switch off at night. Their active brains can take time to slow down, so give

LEFT A corner of a living space is child-friendly, thanks to low chairs and a simple bench. It is now an inviting place to play, draw or read.

ABOVE This large-scale map, pasted directly onto the wall, makes a striking and informative backdrop for a child's desk. Pens and pencils are kept tidy in old tin cans.

them a helping hand by working in subtle, soft light. This can be as simple as fitting a dimmer switch or swapping a high-wattage bulb for a lower one. Alternatively, hang decorative mini lights that produce a soft glow, ideal as a night-light. Always choose LEDs, as they are cool to the touch.

You can have fun with the walls in a child's room, but use a balanced approach to avoid visual chaos. Floral wallpaper looks wonderful on one or two walls, or get your scissors out and cut a tree, car or animal-shape mural from a roll of paper.

A large-scale map, pasted directly to the wall, makes an eye-catching (and educational) alternative to patterned wallpaper – ideal in a boy's room.

When it comes to paint, bold colours are less likely to date than the sugary pinks and pastel blues so often used in younger children's rooms, and they fit in perfectly with the homespun look. Use colour just as you have elsewhere in the homespun home – with balance. The tried and trusted recipe of a neutral backdrop punctuated with pops of pattern and bright colour also translates perfectly to a child's bedroom. Perhaps work in some soothing blues and greens, too, as they are considered to be calming colours for a bedroom.

ABOVE LEFT Pretty fabric bags hung from a painted wooden peg rail make for a colourful display in a child's room. Remember to hang rails low enough for your child to reach, if they are allowed to play with what is hanging up!

ABOVE RIGHT These mobiles are made from fabric remnants and ribbon. Here, they are hung against a wall rather than from the ceiling.

To this well-planned base sprinkle over some homespun magic. Try framing your children's artwork. Their novice attempts at painting can look wonderful when framed and this is a budget alternative to prints or posters. Hang your child's clothes from pegs or hooks, too, to add colour and pattern. Make some bunting – a homespun favourite, it can be stitched by even the novice seamstress from inexpensive remnants. Finally, take a few moments to display favourite pieces, and then store the rest away for a decorative yet uncluttered feel. Teddy bears sitting on a painted chair or a shelf dotted with vintage cars bring homespun style to a room, without stripping it of its child-friendliness.

THIS PAGE Second-hand or junk-store furniture works well in a child's room, because it doesn't matter if it gets bashed about a bit more as your child plays. Here, a drawer unit serves as a bedside table, too, and its chipped blue paintwork brings ready personality. The walls are decorated with favourite clothes hung from hooks and some hand-drawn raindrops in a mix of colours.

Whether you are a passionate maker or just an occasional dabbler, a creative space is a real asset. Few of us can dedicate a whole room to our hobbies, so most creative spaces are tucked into a corner, but these tiny areas can inspire a world of creativity.

creative spaces

Creative spaces can easily become messy, and mess is the enemy of productivity. If you can't lay your hands on the cotton reel or paintbrush you want, when you want it, you will quickly become frustrated. There are aesthetic reasons for keeping your creative space tidy, too. If it is part of another room, it is even more important that you can quickly sort it into an attractive state at the end of a work session. Nobody wants an untidy corner in their peripheral vision when they are trying to relax.

Aim to keep your work surface clutter-free. This means thinking about how you store your tools, fabrics, papers and pencils. They must be to hand, without being in the way. Look for a workstation

LEFT A simple shelf unit above a workspace keeps pens, pencils and brushes that are in regular use conveniently close by.

ABOVE LEFT Neatly rolled and stacked, these pretty trimmings are stored on open shelves.

ABOVE This wire rack has spikes on it for holding cotton reels, allowing them to be stored on a wall where they can be easily seen and accessed.

THIS PAGE This creative space includes a few essential components: storage for materials, a work surface and light from a variety of sources. The tall drawer unit is a vintage French piece, and both the clip light and standard lamp can be positioned to provide strong, directional light.

THIS PAGE Cuttings, photos and tear sheets from magazines and books have been stuck to the wall above this creative space, providing plenty of colourful inspiration. This old office desk has been reinvented as a crafting table, its drawers providing useful storage and its dark wooden colour lifted by the painted orange chair and yellow cushion.

FAR LEFT Rolls of wallpaper are stored upright in a basket to prevent them unravelling.
LEFT An office filing unit on wheels has been given the homespun treatment and brightened up with postcards and pictures pasted onto it.
BELOW Old wooden crates are here used to hold rolls of wool, while vintage tins and glass jars contain smaller materials, such as buttons and beads. A vintage unit with plastic drawers, originally destined for a kitchen, is here used to keep everything from thread to trimmings in order.

that contains some storage. Flea markets and boot fairs/ yard sales are rich hunting grounds. You may stumble across an old clerk's desk with a row of drawers down each side or a no-frills kitchen table with shallow drawers built in. Alternatively, if you need a bespoke table for your creative space, you can construct your own from a piece of wood or toughened glass and trestle legs. Then slide a storage unit on wheels under it that can be pulled out when in use.

Desk drawers alone are unlikely to offer enough storage for the keen crafter, so search second-hand stores for additional furniture for your creative space. You will find attractive chests of drawers and either freestanding or wall-mounted shelving units in abundance, but you may also discover small chests, baskets, magazine racks or handsome filing cabinets. Look out for old shop fittings, too. Display cabinets with lots of drawers or compartments, perhaps once home to the socks or gloves in a department store, can become that indispensable piece of creative-space furniture you were looking for.

Unless you plan to spend all day beavering away at your hobby, a professional, office-style chair is not necessary. Choose instead a simple wooden chair, but check it fits under your chosen workstation. You don't want your legs to be uncomfortably squished against the underside of the table. Wooden chairs, as mentioned elsewhere, are easy to sand down and paint, for a burst of colour. Or simply add a soft cushion in a cheerful shade or pattern. Homespun style is never matchy-matchy, so a bright chair makes a great companion to a dark wooden desk that might otherwise look too heavy.

The wall space immediately around the workstation is where much of your creative kit will live, so think carefully about how you organize it. Shelves are an obvious must-have, to which you can add storage containers or even simple tin cans for

LEFT A brioche pan finds a new life as storage for decorative trimmings.
ABOVE Inspiring images are tacked to the wall behind this workstation and can easily be added to. Paper pom-poms, a lantern strung with ribbon and bunting made from vintage hankies hang from the ceiling and create a playful mood.

holding pencils, paintbrushes, scissors or other tools. Hooks are incredibly helpful, too. Hang small tools or bags containing materials from them, or attach a loop of string to small-scale equipment, like scissors or staplers, so it can be hung up neatly.

The classic homespun concept of finding new ways to display practical objects works particularly well in a creative space. If sewing is your passion, fold and stack your fabric on open shelves so it is always visible. It will become a decorative addition to the room, while also being close at hand for use.

THIS PAGE A simple
trestle table makes
an ideal workstation,
with space beneath
for storage boxes and
baskets. Natural light
from the window
illuminates work by day,
while the anglepoise lamp
provides directional light
at night. An orange chair
and pink lampshade set
the creative tone.

If you have a large collection of vintage wallpaper, store the rolls in an old wire basket or colourful tub by your desk. This is a better way to store them than on a shelf, where they run the risk of unravelling. Keep a collection of cotton reels strung on a wire beneath a shelf so they are easily accessible, and hunt out old jars and canisters for keeping brushes and pencils tidy. Nail food jar lids to the base of a wall-hung shelf, then use the glass jars for storing beads or buttons, unscrewing them as needed.

Lighting is essential to a creative space. Close work like sewing or sketching is impossible without the right light levels. Position your workstation close to a window if you can, to benefit from natural light during the day. For dull days and evening work, you will need artificial light. Basic overhead lighting, perhaps from a central pendant light, is only useful for creating a wash of background light in a creative space, as anything overhead will cause you to cast a dark shadow over your work.

ABOVE The potter behind www.arendal-ceramics.com uses this space to create her beautiful pieces. Floor-to-ceiling shelves hold ceramics that are awaiting decoration.

OPPOSITE Jewellery is made at this creative space, so delicate beads and tiny chain links are kept tidy in tins and glass jars. A pinboard, simply covered in fabric, is a great place to hang completed necklaces, while a simple wooden box is home to ribbon and trimmings. Markets are good hunting grounds for pretty containers, jars and baskets like these.

Instead, choose a task light that can sit on the desk or a wall-mounted shelf. Characterful, second-hand anglepoise-style lights with metal frames and shades crop up at markets and on eBay all the time, and if they are not working, it is easy and inexpensive to have them rewired. With adjustable heads and supports, they offer a flood of flexible, directional light that is ideal for creative work. Look out for inexpensive clip-on lights that you can attach to shelves or the side of your worktop, too. These have the added advantage of taking up no space on your work surface. They are also flexible – you can also easily unclip them and move them around the house, to provide strong light wherever and whenever you need it.

Remember that in a workspace one light source may not be enough, so it is best to invest in a mix of clip-on lights, adjustable lamps and even a freestanding standard lamp with a directional head to guarantee light from a combination of angles.

THIS PAGE This cotton reel rack is a simple but super-useful design, crafted from wire. Paper butterflies stuck to the wall match the colourful cotton it holds. **OPPOSITE** This characterful old cupboard multitasks as a kitchen unit and overflow storage for the house's nearby creative space. Jars of foodstuffs sit on top, while the shelf space and cupboards below hold boxes of fabric and a row of hand-covered notebooks and homemade purses.

Whether you have a tiny terrace, a compact courtyard or rambling country plot, outside space is a valuable addition to any home. It is somewhere to play, read, eat or relax; more an extension of your home than a separate, defined area. So it makes sense to approach it as you would a room in your house. By lifting decorating ideas, colour schemes and even some of the furniture from your homespun home, you can give your garden year-round personality, whatever the weather.

outside living

Good news for anyone lacking green fingers – the homespun outside space doesn't depend on planting for interest and colour. Instead, creating an attractive alfresco environment relies more on how you decorate and furnish the space – whether it is a city courtyard or country patch – than what you grow in it. Simply create an unfussy backdrop to which you can add quirky, junk-store furniture finds, vibrant textiles and a few surprises, too. Glitter ball in a tree, anyone?

Begin by considering the nuts and bolts of your outside space. Are you overlooked? Is there a tree or architectural detail like a pond or shed that you need to work around? Which areas get sunshine?

THIS PAGE This garden overflows with roses, so there are plenty for picking and displaying in pretty china. Folding tables and chairs are ideal, as they can be stored flat out of season. **OPPOSITE** Traditional dining chairs are here used on a terrace. Their slightly austere look is softened by seat pads covered in practical, water-resistant oilcloth and bright cushions.

The answers will help you decide where you position a table, chairs or other seating. In a very sunny garden, commission a carpenter to construct a simple pergola that you can grow plants up, to create some leafy shade. Alternatively, suspend a sail awning over the space in a tough, colourful canvas.

In a small courtyard, increase the feeling of space by hanging a large mirror on one wall. This will also bounce light around and create interesting reflections, while any plant grown in front of it will look twice as verdant. Paint brickwork or woodwork in vibrant shades, too, for year-round colour.

ABOVE & OPPOSITE
A large greenhouse has been converted into a sunny outside room at the heart of this lush, beautiful garden. Despite being outdoors, it has been decorated in much the same way as a room inside would be, with colourful rugs, second-hand furniture and lots of comfortable, hand-stitched cushions.

We often associate certain furniture styles and materials with an outdoor living space. Rattan sofas and café-style chairs are staples of many terraces, but the homespun look likes to tweak convention and think fluidly about what works outside. Old farmhouse chairs or metal stools look fabulous with a touch of homespun styling. Simply paint woodwork with a tough, exterior satin or eggshell and re-cover seats in a bright fabric. Alternatively, forget the makeover and pick up battered old chairs at boot/yard sales specifically for outdoor use. It matters far less if these bargain buys get rained on.

The quality of furniture you choose will depend largely on your available storage space. Where will you keep everything out of season? Winter cold and rain can damage even hard woods like teak, so adequate storage is important. Folding chairs and tables tend to take up less space, or seek out stacking chairs that can be piled up and then stored in a neat tower.

If room is tight inside, invest in a shed or have a small store cupboard built in an unused corner. When painted with a bright finish it will become a cheerful

ABOVE LEFT A mirror hung on a boundary fence helps this small courtyard appear bigger. For an extra shot of colour, its frame has been painted vibrant pink, to match the tablecloth.

ABOVE CENTRE & OPPOSITE ABOVE With holes pierced in its base, a tin can makes an excellent plant pot. On this terrace, colour is supplied by furnishings rather than the planting.

addition to your outdoor space. If you are having seating built in, make sure it contains storage underneath, too. If storage space just can't be found inside or out, ditch the idea of outside furniture and simply use your existing pieces. Move them outdoors when the sun shines, then bring them back in again at night.

Textiles are valuable ingredients of any homespun space. Outside, colourful cushions can soften up a simple built-in bench and a bright cloth will conceal a weather-beaten table. Rugs and mats are equally useful, softening hard paving, injecting colour and helping to zone a space. That simple combination of a rug, low table and comfortable seating creates a distinct relaxation zone and a focal point in what may be a large outside space.

As with inside your home, it is the decorative items that really bring some homespun style. Hang plates on walls or trellises.

Dot a table with freshly cut flowers casually arranged in glass jars or hang cheery bunting from tree branches. Find new ways to show off the familiar, too. Terracotta plant pots are fine, but why not go for something more homespun in flavour? Old food cans, metal buckets and china cups can all hold plants – pick some up when you next visit a flea market. If you can pierce the underside to aid drainage, so much the better.

To enjoy your outside space after the sun has set, work in some atmospheric lighting. A row of bulbs woven loosely through a tree looks festive, but candles will do just as well and are wonderfully romantic. To prevent them blowing out, pop tea lights into old glass jars or hang them in lanterns. Pillar candles can be protected by storm lanterns, or buy specialist outdoor tapers that you can push into the ground. These often come with citronella added; its lemony-sharp scent is designed to keep mosquitoes away so that you can dine in peace.

PREVIOUS PAGES A collection of simple, painted wooden furniture gives this outside space a relaxed, homespun feel. Seat pads, cushions and even vintage quilts help to make the chairs more comfortable and inviting, ideal for a lazy afternoon. A large parasol offers much-needed shade on hot, sunny days. The fresh cut flowers can be taken inside at the end of the day.

OPPOSITE ABOVE LEFT A gravel courtyard gets homespun style with elegant metal seating and a table topped with a purple and pink floral sarong. Coloured lights hung from the trees create a festive atmosphere at night.

OPPOSITE BELOW LEFT Bunting is a favourite of the homespun scheme, and lends an instant party vibe to this outside eating space, whatever the weather! A beautiful bell jar keeps cakes bug-free.

ABOVE This sunroom has a relaxed, rustic feel thanks to the flagstone floor and wooden beams. Potted plants thrive in this light, sunny space and unassuming wooden furniture is completely hidden beneath beautiful fabrics and cushions.

RIGHT A small cabin can become a cosy retreat for both children and adults. This one is decorated with a simple mix of white-painted walls, colourful textiles and flowering plants.

sources

Selina Lake
Stylist & Interiors Author
+44 (0)7971 447785
www.selinalake.co.uk
www.selinalake.blogspot.com

UK & EUROPE
Abigail Brown
www.abigail-brown.co.uk
Designer/maker and illustrator, who mostly works in fabric and stitch. Abigail also creates lovely little fabric birds.

All The Luck In The World
www.alltheluckintheworld.nl
Handmade, vintage and restyled homewares by Jane Schouten.

Bold & Noble
www.boldandnoble.com
Beautiful screen prints made in England, including 'LOVE' and 'Made Do & Mend' prints.

Cable&Cotton
www.cableandcotton.co.uk
Design your own string lights in the colours of your choice.

Drink Shop Do.
9 Caledonian Road
London N1 9DX
www.drinkshopdo.com
Design shop and café. Sells products from emerging designers alongside vintage furniture. Open for lunch, tea and 'cocktail o'clock'; they also host many crafty events and workshops.

Fancy Moon
www.fancymoon.co.uk
Fine fabrics, many with quirky or vintage-inspired patterns.

Folly & Glee
www.follyandglee.co.uk
Cute pre-loved and homemade items, including crochet hangers, lampshades, seasonal decorations and baker's twine.

HobbyCraft
www.hobbycraft.co.uk
Arts and crafts superstores throughout the UK. Visit the website for details of your nearest store.

Liberty
Regent Street
London W1B 5AH
www.liberty.co.uk
+44 (0)20 7734 1234
One of London's oldest department stores selling innovative and eclectic design, and with a wonderful haberdashery department.

The Loft
Tea by the Sea
Loft A
Woodrolfe Road
Tollesbury
Maldon
Essex CM9 8SE
www.t-bythesea.blogspot.com
A modern tearoom with vintage feel, well worth a visit.

Lulu & Nat
www.luluandnat.com
Colourful Indian-inspired and handcrafted textile products, including bedding and rugs.

Petra Boase
www.petraboase.com
Eclectic mix of products: mugs, fabric prints, notebooks and childrenswear.

Pip Studio
www.pipstudio.com/en
Vibrant Dutch designs, including bedding, textiles, wallpaper, porcelain and stationery.

Rice
www.rice.dk
Brightly coloured melamine kitchenware, embroidered cushions and woven floor mats.

Rie Elise Larsen
www.rieeliselarsen.dk
Danish brand specializing in pretty paper lampshades, colourful hooks, porcelain lamps and lovely textiles.

Toast
www.toast.co.uk
Lovely textural homeware with a modern country flavour.

Tsé & Tsé
www.tse-tse.com
French designers of multi-coloured standing lamps, furniture and accessories.

The Yvestown Shop
www.yvestown.com/shop
Handmade crochet scarves, cushion covers and yarns.

USA
Amy Butler
www.amybutlerdesign.com
Pretty printed fabrics, gorgeous organic bedding, home goods and wallpapers.

Anthropologie
www.anthropologie.com
Unique ceramics and glassware with products sourced from around the world. Stores across USA as well as a store in Scotland and two in London.

Grand Revival Design
www.grandrevivaldesign.com
Pretty vintage-inspired fabrics designed by Tanya Whelan.

Grandiflora Home & Garden
719 Grover St,
Lynden WA 98264
+1 360 318 8854
www.grandiflorahome.com
Lovely shop selling vintage pieces and vintage-inspired items for the home and garden.

Heartfish Press
www.heartfishpress.com
New York-based design and letterpress studio producing bold, colourful prints, posters and greetings cards.

Nest Pretty Things

www.nestprettythings.com
*Handmade jewellery and hair
accessories in pastel colours.*

Rifle Paper Co.

www.riflepaperco.com
*Florida-based design studio
producing hand-painted
illustrations, gorgeous,
whimsical stationery and prints.*

Shanna Murray

www.shannamurray.com
*Artist and illustrator who
produces sweet garland design
chalkboards.*

Urban Outfitters

www.urbanoutfitters.com
*Quirky home details and
furnishings with stores throughout
the USA and Europe.*

ONLINE
All Things Original

www.allthingsoriginal.com
*Selling gifts from established
and up-and-coming designers.
Homespun favourites include
Cassia Beck, Heart Zeena, Clare
Nicolson and Showpony.*

DaWanda

www.dawanda.com
*Online marketplace where people
with a passion for unique and
creative products buy and sell.
Homespun favourites include
Jasna's fabric-covered notebooks
and Enna's woodland stationery.*

Epla

www.epla.no
*Norwegian online store for people
buying and selling handmade
items, including Fjeldborg's
patchwork cushions and colourful
furniture by Vivoli Interior.*

Etsy

www.etsy.com
*Online marketplace for small
businesses and craftspeople selling
homemade and vintage items,
Homespun favourites include
Rosehip's amazing crochet-trim
pillowcases, Inspire Lovely's
ribbons and trims, Dottie Angel's
homesewn delights, Ollie Bollen's
Vintage Fabrics and ribbons and
Ninainvorm's ceramics.*

Folksy

www.folksy.com
*UK-based website that acts as a
showcase for talented makers and
their work. Handmade pieces and
crafting supplies bought and sold.*

Pinterest

www.pintrest.com
*Pinterest is a virtual pinboard
that allows you to organize and
share all the beautiful things you
find on the web. You can browse
pinboards created by other people
to discover new things and find
inspiration from people with
shared interests.*
pinterest.com/selinalake/

Poppytalk Handmade

www.poppytalkhandmade.com
*Monthly online street market
where you can sell your own
designs or buy handmade goods
by design talent from all around
the world.*

UGUiSU

http://uguisu.ocnk.net
*Japanese paper goods and
stationery, including Washi tape,
art papers, paper balloons and
cute rubber stamps.*

INSPIRING BLOGS

acreativemint.typepad.com
ariannainteriors.blogspot.com
brightbazaar.blogspot.com
candypopimages.com
cassiab.blogspot.com
creaturecomfortsblog.com
decor8blog.com
designsponge.com
desiretoinspire.net
dottieangel.blogspot.com
eatdrinkchic.com
frydogdesign.blogspot.com
girlwhimsy.blogspot.com
kristybee.blogspot.com
lanaloustyle.blogspot.com
lattelisa.blogspot.com
moderncountry.blogspot.com
molliemakes.themakingspot.
com/blog
oncewed.com
patchworkharmony.blogspot.com
purestyleonline.com
rosehip.typepad.com
ruffledblog.com
secretsofabutterfly.typepad.com
style-files.com
talesoftedandagnes.blogspot.com
teaforjoy.blogspot.com
thatshappy.blogspot.com
toriejayne.blogspot.com
trishabrinkdesign.blogspot.com
yvestown.com

picture credits

Endpapers The Glasgow home of textile designer Fiona Douglas of bluebellgray; 1 The home of Jeanette Lunde; 2 The Paris home of the designer Myriam de Loor, owner of Petit Pan; 3 www.flickr.com/photos/jasnajanekovic/; 4 The home of 'créatrice' and designer Stine Weirsøe Holm in Malmö; 5 The Paris home of the designer Myriam de Loor, owner of Petit Pan; 6 The home of 'créatrice' and designer Stine Weirsøe Holm in Malmö; 7 The London home of stylist Selina Lake (selinalake.blogspot.com); 8–9 The home of Inger Lill Skagen in Norway; 10 The London home of stylist Selina Lake (selinalake.blogspot.com); 11 The family home of Shella Anderson, Tollesbury, UK; 12 The London home of stylist Selina Lake (selinalake.blogspot.com); 13 left and right www.flickr.com/photos/jasnajanekovic/; 13 centre The home of Vidar and Ingrid Aune Westrum; 14 above and 15 The home of Lea Nortved Pedersen, owner of Butik NØ, in Copenhagen; 14 below The Glasgow home of textile designer Fiona Douglas of bluebellgray; 16 above The home of Inger Lill Skagen in Norway; 16 below The home of Vidar and Ingrid Aune Westrum; 17 above Lykkeoglykkeliten.blogspot.com; 17 below rwww.flickr.com/photos/jasnajanekovic/; 18 left The home of Fifi Mandirac in Paris; 18 right The home of Jeanette Lunde; 19 above left The home of Vidar and Ingrid Aune Westrum; 19 above right The family home of Shella Anderson, Tollesbury, UK; 19 below left The home of Inger Lill Skagen in Norway; 19 below right The home of Lea Nortved Pedersen, owner of Butik NØ, in Copenhagen; 20 The London home of stylist Selina Lake (selinalake.blogspot.com); 21–22 The Glasgow home of textile designer Fiona Douglas of bluebellgray; 23 left The Paris home of the designer Myriam de Loor, owner of Petit Pan; 23 centre The home of Fifi Mandirac in Paris; 23 right The home of Inger Lill Skagen in Norway; 24–25 left The Glasgow home of textile designer Fiona Douglas of bluebellgray; 25 right Arendal Keramik www.arendal-ceramics.com; 26 above left The home of Fifi Mandirac in Paris; 26 above right & below The home of Inger Lill Skagen in Norway; 27 The home of Inger Lill Skagen in Norway; 28 above left The family home of Lea Bawnager, Vayu Robins and Elliot Bawnager-Robins, owner of affär; 28 above right Lykkeoglykkeliten.blogspot.com; 28 below left The home of Lea Nortved Pedersen, owner of Butik NØ, in Copenhagen; 28 below right The Paris home of the designer Myriam de Loor, owner of Petit Pan; 29 Lykkeoglykkeliten. blogspot.com; 30 The London home of stylist Selina Lake (selinalake.blogspot.com); 31 The family home of Shella Anderson, Tollesbury, UK; 32 & 33 left The home of Vidar and Ingrid Aune Westrum; 33 centre www.flickr.com/photos/jasnajanekovic/; 33 right The home of 'créatrice' and designer Stine Weirsøe Holm in Malmö; 34 above & below right The home of Jeanette Lunde; 34 below left & 35 The home of Vidar and Ingrid Aune Westrum; 36 The family home of Shella Anderson, Tollesbury, UK; 37 above left & right The home of Vidar and Ingrid Aune Westrum; 37 below left www.flickr.com/photos/jasnajanekovic/; 38–39 The Glasgow home of textile designer Fiona Douglas of bluebellgray; 40 The London home of stylist Selina Lake (selinalake.blogspot.com); 41 www.flickr.com/photos/jasnajanekovic/; 42 The Glasgow home of textile designer Fiona Douglas of bluebellgray; 43 left The Paris home of the designer Myriam de Loor, owner of Petit Pan; 43 centre The home of designer Niki Jones in Glasgow's West End; 43 right The home of Vidar and Ingrid Aune Westrum; 44–45 The home of Inger Lill Skagen in Norway; 46 The home of Vidar and Ingrid Aune Westrum; 47 left The family home of Shella Anderson, Tollesbury, UK; 47 right Lykkeoglykkeliten. blogspot.com; 48–49 The home of designer Niki Jones in Glasgow's West End; 50 The London home of stylist Selina Lake (selinalake.blogspot.com); 51 The home of Fifi Mandirac in Paris; 52 The home of Jeanette Lunde; 53 left The family home of Lea Bawnager, Vayu Robins and Elliot Bawnager-Robins, owner of affär; 53 centre The home of Fifi Mandirac in Paris; 53 right Lykkeoglykkeliten.blogspot.com; 54 The family home of Lea Bawnager, Vayu Robins and Elliot Bawnager-Robins, owner of affär; 55 Lykkeoglykkeliten.blogspot.com; 56 Arendal Keramik www.arendal-ceramics.com; 57 above left The home of Inger Lill Skagen in Norway; 57 above centre The Glasgow home of textile designer Fiona Douglas of bluebellgray; 57 above right The home of Vidar and Ingrid Aune Westrum; 57 below left The home of Lea Nortved Pedersen, owner of Butik NØ, in Copenhagen; 57 below centre Lykkeoglykkeliten.blogspot.com; 57 below right The home of 'créatrice' and designer Stine Weirsøe Holm in Malmö; 58 left The home of Vidar and Ingrid Aune Westrum; 58–59 The Paris home of the designer Myriam de Loor, owner of Petit Pan; 60 The London home of stylist Selina Lake (selinalake.blogspot.com); 61 The home of Jeanette Lunde; 62 & 63 above centre and right The home in Glasgow of textile designer Fiona Douglas of bluebellgray; 63 above left Arendal Keramik www.arendal-ceramics.com; 64 left Lykkeoglykkeliten.blogspot.com; 64 above right The home of Fifi Mandirac in Paris; 64 below right The home of Lea Nortved Pedersen, owner of Butik NØ, in Copenhagen; 65 Lykkeoglykkeliten. blogspot.com; 66 The family home of Shella Anderson, Tollesbury, UK; 67 left & below right The home of Lea Nortved Pedersen, owner of Butik NØ, in Copenhagen; 67 above right Arendal Keramik www.arendal-ceramics.com; 68 above www.flickr.com/photos/jasnajanekovic/; 68 below left The home of Vidar and Ingrid Aune Westrum; 68 below left The Glasgow home of textile designer Fiona Douglas of bluebellgray; 69 The home of Inger Lill Skagen in Norway; 70–71 The home of Vidar and Ingrid Aune Westrum; 72 above left Lykkeoglykkeliten.blogspot.com; 72 above right The home of Fifi

Mandirac in Paris; **72 below & 73** The Glasgow home of textile designer Fiona Douglas of bluebellgray; **74–75** The home of Jeanette Lunde; **76–77** Designer Lisa Stickley; **78** The family home of Lea Bawnager, Vayu Robins and Elliot Bawnager-Robins, owner of affär; **80–81** Arendal Keramik www.arendal-ceramics.com; **82–83** The home of Inger Lill Skagen in Norway; **84 above left & below** The home of Lea Nortved Pedersen, owner of Butik NØ, in Copenhagen; **84 above right** The Paris home of the designer Myriam de Loor, owner of Petit Pan; **85** Arendal Keramik www.arendal-ceramics.com; **86** www.flickr.com/photos/jasnajanekovic/; **87** The home of Vidar and Ingrid Aune Westrum; **88** The Paris home of the designer Myriam de Loor, owner of Petit Pan; **89 above left** The family home of Shella Anderson, Tollesbury, UK; **89 above right** The home of 'créatrice' and designer Stine Weirsøe Holm in Malmö; **89 below** The Paris home of the designer Myriam de Loor, owner of Petit Pan; **90 above left** Arendal Keramik www.arendal-ceramics.com; **90 above centre & right** The home of Lea Nortved Pedersen, owner of Butik NØ, in Copenhagen; **90 below left** The home of Lea Nortved Pedersen, owner of Butik NØ, in Copenhagen; **90 below right** The home of Vidar and Ingrid Aune Westrum; **91** The home of Lea Nortved Pedersen, owner of Butik NØ, in Copenhagen; **92 & 93 left** The family home of Shella Anderson, Tollesbury, UK; **93 right** The home of Inger Lill Skagen in Norway; **94 above left** Arendal Keramik www.arendal-ceramics.com; **94–95** www.flickr.com/photos/jasnajanekovic/; **96–97** The family home of Lea Bawnager, Vayu Robins and Elliot Bawnager-Robins, owner of affär; **98–99** The home of Jeanette Lunde; **100–101** The home of 'créatrice' and designer Stine Weirsøe Holm in Malmö; **102–103 above** The home of Inger Lill Skagen in Norway; **102 below** The home of Vidar and Ingrid Aune Westrum; **104 above left & below** Designer Lisa Stickley; **104 above right & 105** Lykkeoglykkeliten.blogspot.com; **106 above** The Glasgow home of textile designer Fiona Douglas of bluebellgray; **106 below** The home of Inger Lill Skagen in Norway; **107** The home of 'créatrice' and designer Stine Weirsøe Holm in Malmö; **108** The family home of Shella Anderson, Tollesbury, UK; **109** Designer Lisa Stickley; **110–111** The home of Jeanette Lunde; **112–113** The home of Vidar and Ingrid Aune Westrum; **113 above right** The home of Fifi Mandirac in Paris; **114–115** The home of designer Niki Jones in Glasgow's West End; **116 left** The home of designer Niki Jones in Glasgow's West End; **116 centre** The home of Lea Nortved Pedersen, owner of Butik NØ, in Copenhagen; **116 right** Arendal Keramik www.arendal-ceramics.com; **117–118** The family home of Shella Anderson, Tollesbury, UK; **119 above left** The home of Vidar and Ingrid Aune Westrum; **119 right** The family home of Shella Anderson, Tollesbury, UK; **119 below left** Lykkeoglykkeliten.blogspot.com; **120** The home of designer Niki Jones in Glasgow's West End;

121 above The home of 'créatrice' and designer Stine Weirsøe Holm in Malmö; **121 below** The family home of Shella Anderson, Tollesbury, UK; **122–125** The family home of Shella Anderson, Tollesbury, UK; **126 & 127 left** Lykkeoglykkeliten.blogspot.com; **127 right** The home of 'créatrice' and designer Stine Weirsøe Holm in Malmö; **127 below** The home of Jeanette Lunde; **128 above right** The home of Fifi Mandirac in Paris; **128–129 below** The home of Jeanette Lunde; **130** The home of Fifi Mandirac in Paris; **131** The family home of Lea Bawnager, Vayu Robins and Elliot Bawnager-Robins, owner of affär; **132–133** www.flickr.com/photos/jasnajanekovic/; **134 above left** The home of the designer Myriam de Loor, owner of Petit Pan in Paris; **134 above right** www.flickr.com/photos/jasnajanekovic/; **134 below & 135** The Paris home of the designer Myriam de Loor, owner of Petit Pan; **136–137** Lykkeoglykkeliten.blogspot.com; **138** The London home of stylist Selina Lake (selinalake.blogspot.com); **138 below** The home of Jeanette Lunde; **139** The home of 'créatrice' and designer Stine Weirsøe Holm in Malmö; **140** Arendal Keramik www.arendal-ceramics.com; **141–143** www.flickr.com/photos/jasnajanekovic/; **144** The family home of Shella Anderson, Tollesbury, UK; **145–147** Arendal Keramik www.arendal-ceramics.com; **148–149** The family home of Shella Anderson, Tollesbury, UK; **150–151** Arendal Keramik www.arendal-ceramics.com; **152 left** The home of Fifi Mandirac in Paris; **152 below & 153** The home of Inger Lill Skagen in Norway; **155** The home of 'créatrice' and designer Stine Weirsøe Holm in Malmö; **157** Arendal Keramik www.arendal-ceramics.com; **160** The London home of stylist Selina Lake (selinalake.blogspot.com).

business credits

Key: a = above; b = below;
r = right; l = left; c = centre

Shella Anderson
The Loft – Tea by the Sea
www.t-bythesea.blogspot.com
*11, 19ar, 31, 36, 47l, 66, 89al,
92, 93l, 108, 117–118, 119ar,
121b, 122–125, 144, 148–149.*

Ingrid G. Aune Westrum
www.fjeldborg.no
www.epla.no/shops/fjeldborg
www.13tretten.no
*13c, 16b, 19a, 32, 33l, 34bl,
35,37al, 37r, 43r, 46, 57ar, 58l,
68bl, 70–71, 87, 90br, 102b,
112–113, 119al.*

Lea Bawnager
affär
www.affaer.dk
facebook.com/affaer
28al, 53l, 54, 78, 96–97, 131.

Fiona Douglas
Bluebellgray
www.bluebellgray.co.uk
*Endpapers, 14b, 21–22, 24,
25l, 38–39, 42, 57ac, 62, 63
ac, 68bl, 72b, 73 106a.*

Tove Michelle Hjallum
www.lykkeoglykkeliten.
blogspot.com
www.nettpynt.no
*17a, 28ar, 29, 47r, 53r, 55,
57bc, 64l, 65, 72al, 104ar, 105,
119bl, 126, 127l, 136–137.*

Jasna Janekovic
www.flickr.com/photos/jasna
janekovic/
www.dawanda.com/shop/jasna
*3, 13l, 13r, 17b, 33c, 37bl, 41,
68a, 86, 94–95, 132–133,
134ar, 141–143.*

Niki Jones
www.niki-jones.co.uk
*43c, 48–49, 114–115, 116l,
120.*

Selina Lake
Stylist and author
+44 (0)7971447785
www.selinalake.co.uk
www.selinalake.blogspot.com
*7,10, 12, 20, 30, 40, 50, 60,
138, 160.*

Rie Elise Larsen APS
www.rieeliselarsen.dk

Susan Liebe
www.liebeshop.dk
*14a, 15, 19br, 28bl, 57bl, 64br,
67l, 67br, 84al, 84b, 90ac, 90r,
90bl, 91, 93r, 116c.*

Myriam de Loor
Petit Pan
7 rue de Prague
75012 Paris
www.petitpan.com
*2, 5, 23l, 28br, 43l, 58–59,
84ar, 88, 89b, 134al, 134b,
135.*

Jeanette Lunde
www.frydogdesign.blogspot.com
*1, 18r, 34a, 34br, 52, 61,
74–75, 98–99k 110–111, 127b,
128, 129b, 138b.*

Fifi Mandirac
www.fifimandirac.com
*18l, 23c, 26al, 51, 53c, 64ar,
762ar, 113ar, 128ar, 130, 152l.*

Lea Nortved Pedersen
Lea Nortved Pedersen
Butik NØ
Larsbjornstraede 22 TV,
1454 Copenhagen
Denmark
T: +45 261 67849
www.butiknØ.dk

Inger Lill Skagen
www.kasparasregnbue.blogspot.
com
*8–9, 16a, 19bl, 23r, 26ar, 26b,
27, 44–45, 57al, 69, 82–83,
102, 103a, 106b, 152b, 153.*

Tsé & Tsé associées
20, rue Moreau
75012 Paris
France
www.tse-tse.com
*2, 5, 23l, 28br, 43l, 58–59,
84ar, 88, 89b, 134al, 134b,
135.*

Stine Weirsøe
www.lutterlagkage.dk
*4, 6, 33r, 57br, 89ar, 100–101,
107, 121a, 127r, 139, 155.*

Jette Arendal Winther
Arendal Keramik
Tverved 10
3390 Hundested
www.arendal-ceramics.com
www.danishcreramics.com
*25r, 56, 63al, 67ar, 80–81,
85, 90al, 94al, 116r, 140,
145–147, 150–151, 157.*

index

acknowledgments

Enormous thanks, Debi Treloar, for your amazing photography, gorgeous friendship and brilliant company especially while we toured Europe…you know I absolutely love working with you!

I would like to thank everyone at Ryland Peters & Small for their hard work and dedication. Megan Smith, I'm thrilled with the design. Jess Walton, many thanks for organizing all the trips: it was amazing working in Norway, Denmark, Sweden, Germany, Paris, London and Essex. Thanks also to Annabel Morgan and Leslie Harrington, and a special thanks to Alison Starling for agreeing to go ahead with my third book.

Massive thanks to all of you who welcomed Debi and I into your homes – we loved meeting you and we both felt hugely inspired by your creativity and homespun ideas. Joanna Simmons, thank you for putting *Homespun Style* into such interesting words.

Thanks go also to all who support my work online and in the press – I really appreciate being mentioned on your websites, blogs and in magazines and books. Also big thanks to those who follow my blog – your kind comments mean a lot to me.

Finally, thank you to all my family, especially Mum and Dad, who have always encouraged my creative side, and my amazing husband Dave – I love you.